The Fun of Figure Skating

THE FUN OF

Illustrations by Robert Riger

Maribel Vinson Owen

Foreword by R. Norman Wood,
Head Hockey Coach, Princeton University

Figure Skating

A PRIMER OF THE ART-SPORT

HARPER & BROTHERS   PUBLISHERS   NEW YORK

To my skating family
Mother, Father, Husband, and Daughters
who have engendered and sustained
my great love of figure skating

Contents

Foreword

by R. Norman Wood
HEAD HOCKEY COACH, PRINCETON UNIVERSITY

If Maribel Owen were asked how long it took her to write *The Fun of Figure Skating,* her reply would have to be "all my life." Figure skating, in the highly competitive way she has known it, has meant year after year of painstaking practice, arduous exercise, and strict training; yet running parallel to this regimen, Mrs. Owen has enjoyed all the relaxing fun of skating with her family and watching her two daughters progress from the beginner's first wobbly steps to a precision and finesse that rivals her own.

This, perhaps, is the true wonder of figure skating as a sport. Unlike ice hockey, which must by its very nature be competitive and which even in hockey-happy families divides the household sharply into male players and distaff spectators, figure skating sets up no barriers as to sex, age, or ability. Perhaps the most dramatic example of this is the annual event, "Ice Chips," a full-scale ice show put on by the Skating Club of Boston. Youngsters scarcely out of the toddling stage skate side by side with "youngsters" of sixty or more, and such famous skaters as Olympic champion David Jenkins share the applause with veritable beginners.

Yet, for the person who genuinely enjoys the rigors of competition, figure skating offers a challenge every bit as demanding as that found in ice hockey or speed skating. Not only is an astounding combination of balance, strength, and coordination required for championship form, but the final result must look effortless, a condition that would severely tax the abilities of the finest speed skater or hockey player. In hockey, for example, getting the puck into the net is the important thing even if you look like an elephant on ice doing it, and mishaps frequently draw praise for over-eagerness rather than criticism for poor form. For my own part, watching some hockey player whose otherwise brilliant performance is marred by his inability to turn adequately in both directions, I have often felt that learning a little of the figure skater's grace would be a distinct advantage in the game, and that figure skating should be given greater consideration as the natural complement to hockey.

Needless to say, I hardly expect to find a second David Jenkins on any team I coach, but who knows, perhaps some of the flawless execution that an Olympian like Jenkins displays might at least bedazzle the opposing goalie so much that he'd let the puck slip through!

Introduction

THIS little book on figure skating is subtitled a "primer" because it is expressly designed to teach the ABC's of a fascinating sport and a new art. It is for all of you who, after seeing the latest ice show, may have decided that skating looks like wonderful fun and you'd like to try it. You may never have been on a pair of skates in your life, or at any rate you may never have been on a pair of figure skates. You may not even know that there is any difference between the kind of skates used for figure skating and those used for plain skating and hockey. Or perhaps you are an ex-hockey player who is finding it difficult to line up other members of a team, or again maybe you are a parent who wants to see your children off to a correct start in this most beneficial of pastimes. At any rate, it is for you, the enthusiastic novice, that this book is mainly written.

However, beyond the description of correct equipment and the right way to take your first few strokes on the ice, there are descriptions of the fundamental figures of skating that should prove useful not only to the beginner but to every student of the sport, no matter how advanced.

A figure skater, even a champion, is no better than his mastery of the primary edges. Teaching thousands of skaters, beginners in groups as well as World and Olympic competitors, has convinced me over and over again, in the twenty-two years that have elapsed since I taught my first pupil, of the incontrovertible truth of that statement. Even though a skater may do double-revolution jumps in the air and spin faster than a whirling dervish, he is not a true skater unless he has the gliding stroke, the effortless speed, the "soft" knee and ankle, the graceful form, and the correct way of putting his skate upon the ice that come only from a thorough education in basic stroking and the first few fundamental figures.

Choppy steps and an unnatural style are usually the result of trying to become an advanced skater too soon. Once the fundamental figures are mastered so that they are done with control, even speed, and correct form, the advanced figures come twice as quickly and they will then automatically be done with control, even speed, and correct form. Walking comes before running. A good primary figure comes before a good advanced figure, and, conversely, a half-mastered primary figure means many half-mastered advanced figures. Therefore, although the figures and moves described in this book are only a small part of figure skating as a whole, they are by far the most important part.

If you learn these primer figures well (and anyone, no matter what age, *can* learn them well), then, depending to a certain degree on your physical limitations but much more on your own capacity for practice, you can become a really accomplished skater capable of giving yourself and others much pleasure by your ability. I am often asked by beginning students: "How *long* will it take me to feel at home on my figure skates?" "When will I be ready to try dancing?" "How long before I'll be able to jump?" Of course there can be no set answer to such queries, but many times I have taught a class of absolute neophytes, who could practice no more than twice a week, to master forward and backward stroking, the crossovers, the basic edge positions, and the simple turns well enough by the end of one season to warrant their starting the preliminary test figures and the simplest of the many ice dances plus, for the young or the daring, the rudimentary jumps.

The hardest part of skating comes within these pages, yet the progression from your first stroke to your first figure and on to your next figure will be so fascinating and so natural that you won't think of it as difficult—you'll just think you're having a wonderful time. For figure skating not only looks like fun, it *is* fun. Interesting and exciting as watching it in shows or on television may be, skating yourself is much more interesting and exciting.

It is first of all a sport, a highly technical sport which is at once healthful and social. Unlike many other sports, you need no partner to enjoy it; if you have a partner, you will have the double fun of pair skating; and if you have many partners, you will be able to dance in turn with all of them. Indeed, it is because dancing on ice is more rhythmic and lilting than dancing on a ballroom floor that a majority of you will don figure skates in the first place and then will keep on skating year after year until your old bones refuse to move any more. As proof let me cite the case of Oscar L. Richard who performed a *solo* in the New York Skating Club carnival in Madison Square Garden at the age of ninety, or that of Philip Sharples of Cambridge who skated a Dutch waltz with his young partner of fifty in the forty-eighth annual Skating Club of Boston "Ice Chips" show in Boston Garden when he was a spry eighty-seven!

Figure skating, like ballet dancing, has its own tenets and strict technicalities. These tenets and technicalities have changed and broadened greatly since the modern, or "international," style of figure skating was adopted in this country approximately fifty years ago. Though ever greater latitude of movement has developed until specialties that would have been frowned on as overly "acrobatic" twenty-five years ago are commonplace today, the fundamentals of figure skating remain unchanged, and it is within them that the greatest artistic expression is possible. The roots of figure skating always have been and, despite the popularity of professional shows, undoubtedly always will be solidly planted in competition, where correct methods of execution and beautiful innovations of movement are retained and fostered.

Figure skating is divided into two parts, the so-called "school figures" and "free skating." School figures, as their name implies, are the basic edges, turns, and changes of edge of which free skating is composed. The figures are two-lobed or three-lobed eights skated alternately on the right and left foot around to a center or starting point. There are forty-two figures in all, including the elementary and the advanced. Nine of these figures are described in this book.

Free skating means long edges—or "spirals"—dance steps, big sweeping turns, jumps, spins, and spread-eagles skated over the whole surface of the ice and in rhythm with music. It is this part of skating that is nearest to the dance and may be made a medium for expressing the skater's individuality and personality, whether he skates alone, in pairs, fours, or carnival groups. This is the part of skating that you as a spectator have enjoyed at exhibitions and shows, and it is the part that you eventually will enjoy to the fullest as you sweep down the ice in your own speedy spirals or leap from the ice in a high, controlled, rhythmic jump.

Perhaps you will never be young enough to do much in the way of jumping or spinning and perhaps you will never have the time or the inclination for any sort of competition, but you will have just as much fun as the jumpers and spinners and the competitors, for you will do all the lovely skating dance steps alone or with expert partners and you will enjoy every minute on the ice.

Back at the beginning of the century Mrs. Edgar Syers of England, the first lady figure skating champion of the world, wrote: "Skating is an exercise fitted for both old and young. It may be taken as an exacting art or merely as a pleasant diversion; but for those who intend to practise for competitions, it has endless attractions. Its difficulties make it all the more interesting. There are always new fields to conquer. From the point of view of health, there are few if any exercises to compare with it; and it has the advantage of being equally fascinating when practised alone or in the delightful form of pair-skating."

What this great lady figure skater claimed for her sport during the early years of its international organization is even truer today.

The Fun of Figure Skating

I

Equipment—No Such Thing as Weak Ankles

Correct equipment is the first and most important element in the making of a good figure skater. You are keen to learn to skate but you have no skates? Or perhaps you'd love to figure skate but you've tried skating a couple of times on a rented or borrowed outfit and have found that you have "weak ankles"? Then you must pay strict attention to the type of boot and skate to buy. Read the following few instructions carefully and follow them out just as carefully.

Boots

Don't allow any salesman to persuade you into buying boots that don't fit you. Unfortunately many salesmen in our sporting goods stores still know very little about the proper fit of a boot for figure skating, and, because it is easier for them or less expensive perhaps for you, they will let you walk out of their store with a much too large outfit or a completely unsuitable one which has been fitted over a heavy sock.

Remember this: The common excuse of weak ankles is not a valid one. It has been proved that not one person in a hundred really has weak ankles if he has properly fitting boots. On the other hand, anyone will have weak ankles in a boot that is too large in the heel and instep. Those of you who have tried skating only in a low, ill-fitting hockey boot and a high hockey skate and who became discouraged because you could not hold your ankles upright must not be discouraged another minute. With a high, close-fitting boot and a low figure skate you will find balancing on the steel runners ever so much easier. After a

1

few turns around the rink you will find that you can hold your ankles in place with a minimum of effort, and after a session or two you will have no difficulty at all.

A figure skating boot is much higher and gives more support than the common hockey boot. A man's boot is about 9 inches high, and a woman's about 8 inches. It must fit so snugly that your heel does not slip up and down the least bit, even when the boot is only loosely laced. The fit through the instep and ankle up to the back of the big toe joint must be equally tight. There should be no wrinkles from the instep back to the heel over the anklebone and, most important, there should be a wide spread of 1 inch to 1½ inches between the lacings over the instep, even when the boot is laced up tight. This wide spread allows for the inevitable stretching of the leather and ensures a good fit for many years of wear. Don't buy a boot with an ankle strap. This really tends to be weakening.

There is one part of the boot, however, that should not be tight—and that is the toe. If possible, see that your boot has a round or square toe; never buy a pointed model. There should be enough space from the big toe joint forward to the end so that you can wiggle your toes freely inside the boot at all times. Tight toes stuffed with heavy socks are the most common reason for cold feet during outdoor skating.

Never have your skating boots fitted over a heavy sock. Women should wear only silk stockings for a fitting, while men should wear their ordinary, everyday socks. For some reason or other would-be skaters and skate salesmen feel that boots fit better and feet will keep warmer with heavy socks. This is far from the truth. In the first place, a boot must fit so well that it feels like a part of your foot after a little while. It is impossible to get this accurate, snug fit over a heavy sock, whereas a boot that has been well fitted over silk stockings will always take a thin sock or tights later on, if desired. In the second place, just as a sock may fill up around the ankle it will also fill up the toe, preventing proper circulation. I have been warm skating outdoors at 20 degrees below zero in a pair of thin tights and a round-toed boot, while skaters around me have rushed inside with numb feet—and, later, painfully burning toes—because they mistakenly thought a heavy sock would give added comfort! *A good rule of thumb is: Skating boots should be a half-size to a whole size smaller than your walking shoes.*

The question of buying boots for children needs special attention. While it is true that most children in the growing stage cannot wear more than one year a pair of skates and boots that fit anywhere near correctly at the time of buying, it is also true that children progress toward good skating faster than their elders, and it is hardly fair to handicap them with ill-fitting equipment. Figure skating, whether outdoors or in, is one of the most healthful and beneficial of all sports for children. It is not too strenuous for their young muscles, yet it gives them complete exercise for almost every muscle of the body, expands the lungs, and develops good posture and fine power of concentration.

Though new outfits yearly may seem expensive on first thought, it is a shame to start children off on boots and skates so large that they lose interest in trying to control their ankles. I have seen this happen to many eager children, and it is too bad. I have also seen that there is almost always a ready market for children's outgrown outfits. If you buy little John a pair of boots and skates that really fit him this year and he has outgrown them by next fall, you will find that Mrs. Smith will be only too delighted to buy a still good outfit for less than she would have to pay for a new one in the stores. At many of the rinks skate shops and professionals conduct a regular barter and exchange counter for youngsters' outfits. If you don't live near a rink, I think you'll find it easy to set up your own exchange.

Skates

Now that you've been fitted properly to your boots, skates are the next consideration. Strangely enough, your skates, while important, are not so important as your boots. A pair of low figure skates of the correct size and shape does not have to be expensive or even moderately expensive to be perfectly satisfactory for a long while. I skated for several years and learned all my fundamental figures on ordinary five dollar figure skates, which today would cost approximately ten dollars.

So that you will know for yourself whether you are being sold the right blades, pick up the skates on the counter and examine them carefully. Ask for a hockey skate and hold it in your left hand. Now ask for a figure skate and hold it in your right hand. The first thing you will notice is that the hockey skate has a plain pointed end in front, while the figure skate has a series of "teeth," or "picks." Hold the plate of the skates in your hands with the blades facing upward, and turn the blades to the light. You will notice that the hockey skate, in your left hand, has an absolutely straight narrow blade—that is, the length of the blade is straight from heel to toe and the width of the blade is perfectly straight across. Now look at the figure blade. You will notice that from heel to toe the blade is set on a slight curve. This is called the "radius" of the skate, and most figure skates today are set on a 7-foot radius.

Look at and feel the blade itself. (Illus. 1). You will notice that there is a hollow ridge down the center of the skate, leaving two higher edges at each side of it (see insert). This hollow ridge is called the "concave" of the skate and is what is meant by the term "hollow-ground" as applied to figure skates. The sides of the hollow ridge are the so-called "edges" of the skate, and when you have your outfit on, the edge of the skate that is nearest the inside of your foot is called the "inside edge," and the edge nearest the outside is correspondingly called the "outside edge." It is well to memorize these terms, for the actual skating figures are named according to which edge of the skate you use to trace them.

To get back to the skates you are holding in your hands— grasp the blades firmly, with the skates perfectly level and near together. You will immediately notice that the shoe plate of the hockey skate is higher than that of the figure skate, and if you look more closely, you will see that the two upright pieces that join the toe plate and the heel plate to the blade (in other words, the "stanchions") are much higher on the hockey skate than on the figure skate. This is important. The higher your foot is from the ice, the harder it is to keep your ankle upright. It is much the same principle as stilt walking; the lower your center of gravity, naturally the easier it is to balance.

Therefore it stands to reason that it is easier to learn to skate

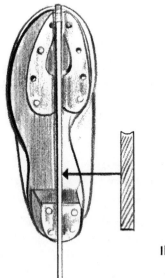

Illustration 1

on the low figure skates than on the high hockey skates. Even if you are not sure you ever want to try figures, even if you think you will be content to plain skate round and round the village pond or city rink, you will find it ever so much easier to learn to navigate over the ice on figure skates. You can play everything except top drawer hockey on figure skates, but you can never trace even the simplest figures correctly or dance an ice waltz on hockey skates.

One last important item: See that your skates are fastened to your boot slightly inside the center line that runs from toe to heel. (Illus. 1) This puts the skate where the body weight is greatest and also will enable you to skate on the outside edge more easily later on. Buy skates of such a length that the toe plate comes forward exactly to the end of the boot. Skates made all in one piece, with the teeth fastened to the toe plate, are strongest. Unless your skates come already fastened to the boots, it is well to have an expert do the attaching. If the skates are already attached to the boots, as is the case in most department and sporting goods stores, *make sure* that they are attached by *screws, not rivets*. This is vitally important. The placing of a riveted skate cannot be changed without ruining the sole of the boot; a skate that is screwed on can be changed at any skate shop to adjust to your individual balance. Most factories set the skate on the sole of the boot in the wrong alignment, and it is necessary to change in the majority of cases. Screwed on skates, not riveted, please.

Another item that should be purchased at this time is a good skate guard of wood, rubber, or plastic. It won't matter how fine an outfit you have if you step on anything but ice in your skates. Concrete, steel, even wood unless it is clean, will ruin the edge of your blade in a second or two. Wear your guards to the ice and when you leave the ice, put them on right there. Rust is likewise an enemy of your skate. After each use wipe your blades carefully (a chamois is best), and do not put them back in your guards again until you are certain the inside of each guard is completely dry. Sharpening should be done at a skating rink or wherever a skate shop has the right type of grinding wheel for figure skates. Beware of the average hardware or sporting goods store; they rarely have the correct sharpening equipment. At any rate, make inquiries before handing over your skates. One more caution: Never have the teeth removed.

Price

I have left the vital question of price to the last. Figure skating, long regarded as an expensive sport, is becoming less expensive all the time. Stores are stocking better and cheaper equipment every year. Furthermore, even an outfit that seems expensive at first will last so long, if it is well made of good materials, that the cost in the end will seem negligible. If you are to be the run-of-the-mill type of "weekend" skater, who skates for fun and relaxation only, a good pair of boots and skates will probably last you most of your skating life. This is particularly true of men's black boots. Even women's white buck or calf boots will last many seasons. I strongly advise buying the best outfit you can possibly afford, because it is economy in the end.

However, if you don't want to spend much yet for a sport you're not sure you're going to like (though of course you will!), it is possible to get a satisfactory outfit for as little as twenty-five dollars for adults and fifteen dollars for children—satisfactory, that is, so long as you are particular about the fit. If you are one of those people whom no cheap boot will really fit properly, do pay a little extra for a better cut boot which comes in a greater range of sizes and widths. You will find that you are more than repaid in comfort and pleasure. If you can not be fitted by any ready-made boot, it is wise to pay for the best custom-made pair you can get. I say again, and I can't emphasize it too strongly, that the fit of the boot is the most important factor in your first season on the ice.

Skating Clothes

After you have acquired your boots and skates, your thoughts will turn naturally to the clothes you will wear for your first appearance. Make no mistake about it, a smart costume on the ice is half the battle. If you are a man, you will probably decide to do your first skating in long trousers plus an ordinary coat or sweater, and that is all right. If you are a woman and an absolute beginner and expect to do a certain amount of rail clinging for a while, you will probably think you will be less conspicuous in a long skirt, a sort of modified street costume. There you are wrong.

For a woman the traditional costume is as set for the ice rink as it is for the tennis court or the ski slope. A long skirt will make any woman stand out like a sore thumb on any ice surface, just as a long black skirt would make her an object of special attention on any tennis court. So remember this when you buy your costume: if you want your first few wobbly strokes to go as unnoticed as possible, be sure to dress in the accepted mode. If you dress like a reasonably expert skater (whether you are or not), you'll find that people are much too preoccupied with their own edges to pay any attention to yours.

The accepted style for skating skirts and dresses has a full circular, gored, or pleated skirt which flares from the hipline. Plenty of stores now have the most chic, correct, and practical costumes imaginable—and at very small cost. In fact it is because the stores are putting out such attractive and becoming figure skating outfits that lots of young girls are taking up the sport!

As for the rest of the costume, good sense and a certain amount of fashion should dictate. Sweaters with skirts are always good, but if you are going to an indoor rink, don't make the mistake, as one of my friends did, of wearing a heavy sweater, a stocking cap, and fur-lined mitts. Most rinks are heated nowadays, so it is well to inquire first. On the other hand, trim windbreakers, parkas, and turtleneck sweaters are perfect for pond skating. Big hats are out of place on the ice. The closer fitting the cap, the trimmer the appearance. Streamlining is as suitable to the skating figure as it is to an automobile chassis.

Anything that doesn't contribute to an impression of speed and freedom of movement is undesirable. That is why the bodices of skating dresses should be molded to the figure. That is why trunks should never be large and bulky—but, contrariwise the too tight, too high little panty that some good skaters are now affecting is ugly, too. Trunks should as a general rule match the skirt and be as inconspicuous as possible. Excellent nylon tights are available at most stores, while wool and nylon tights may also be procured. The latter are fine for outdoor skating in cold climates.

Many beginners don slacks for their first appearances on the ice. This is a practical costume, but as ability increases, a skirt gives not only more freedom but a great deal more grace.

Be sure that your skating dress is made with a gusset under the arms to allow full latitude of movement and at the same time a tight fit in the bodice—and the sleeve, too, if desired.

One of the most satisfactory of all costumes for both indoor and outdoor skating is the knitted dress. Jersey is also good for free and easy movement.

Simplicity of line and effectiveness of color are the important items in a successful costume. Any decoration should enhance rather than clutter the line of the skater's body. A good rule of thumb for skirt length is this: Bend forward from the hips with both legs straight under you and have your hemline marked at the exact point where your upper leg meets your derrière.

For men there are now well-cut, tight-fitting trousers on sale at most stores. Some rinks make the wearing of coats compulsory, but sweaters are best outdoors. As with the ladies, men should aim for the trim, uncluttered line, comfortable through the arm and shoulders but, please, not baggy or sloppy anywhere—pants leg, waistline, or neckline. Clothes may not make the man but on the ice they certainly help to make a better-looking skater.

II

First Strokes on the Ice

Now that you are properly shod and clothed for the ice, the next step is on the ice itself. But wait—there is one more set of instructions before you stroke off on that gleaming surface. There is a right way and a wrong way of lacing up your boots, so pause an extra moment on the sidelines and make sure that yours are done up right. Many a first-time skater has come off the ice after a few minutes complaining of cramps in his legs or feet merely because he didn't know that there was a special art in bootlacing for comfort.

The lace should be left fairly loose in the first few eyelets from the toe almost to the instep bone (remember the "wiggle-toe" principle), but from the instep bone across the ankle, as far as the first or second eyelet above the anklebone, you should pull the laces *just as tight as you can* (Illus. 2). Now tie a surgeon's knot—that is, hold one lacing and wrap the other one twice around it, pulling the ends tight. From this point to the top of the boot make your lacings quite loose.

The surgeon's knot will hold your ankle laces tight, but if you continue them tight up your calf, you will have cramped muscles without fail. I test my own lacing by inserting two fingers inside the top of the boot; then I know I shall be free to bend deeply and exercise hard without fear of cramping. From the surgeon's knot to the boot top you should have the labor-saving device of eyelet hooks; and if your boots don't have them, any cobbler will attach them for a small sum. The days of interminable lacing plus cold blue fingers at the pond's edge are luckily over.

10

YOUR FIRST TIME ON THE ICE

At last you are quite ready for your first skate. Step onto the ice with the aid of a rail or a friend's hand and stand still in a relaxed position, your feet parallel about 6 inches apart, with both ankles upright and your weight evenly distributed. Now bend both knees and both ankles *forward,* making sure that your pelvis stays *forward* over your feet and the rest of the body

Illustration 2

upright with your back straight but not arched, your shoulders easy, and head erect. This is the basic *posture of skating* (Illus. 3-A) and ensures that the weight of the body is directly over the skates. It is essentially the posture of walking plus an exaggerated forward bend of the ankles which puts the points of your knees so far ahead of the points of your skates that if you look down in this position, *without "dropping" your head or shoulders over,* you should not be able to see your feet at all. Flex your knees and ankles gently a few times to get used to the feel of so much bending. If you are a skier, this won't feel

A

B

Illustration 3

strange to you; if a non-skier, you may feel a tightness at the back of your heels. In that case there are stretching exercises which I shall prescribe for you shortly.

With your feet still parallel and your knees still bent, but *without moving your feet at all,* turn your right ankle first in, then out. Do the same with your left. As you turn each one in, you have automatically turned over onto the edge of the blade nearer the center of the body, or onto the "inside edge." As you turn each ankle out, or away from the center of your body, you are on the "outside edge" of your skate. Be sure to memorize these terms, for everything we do in figure skating is named from them. When your ankle is perfectly upright, you are then on both edges evenly, or the "flat" of your skate.

Still with the assistance of the rail or the kind friend's hand, try moving gently forward, balancing first on one blade and then the other. Be sure to try hard to keep your ankles perfectly upright and straight underneath you. Remember the only ankle-bending in skating is *forward.* This is so vitally important that I shall reiterate it many times before our lessons are completed. As you balance on your right foot, lift the left a short way straight up beside it. Then put the left straight down *close beside* the right in a sort of "mark time" movement, shifting all your body weight to the left and gently lifting the right foot straight up as you make the change. I call these "baby steps," (Illus. 4) and they are very useful in teaching you the feel of one-skate balance. *They also teach you the important fundamental that it is easier to catch an accurate balance each time you change feet if your new stroke starts directly beside and close to the old one.*

DOUBLE SCULLING

When you have gained a bit of confidence from baby stepping, it is time for you to try propelling yourself over the ice alone. To keep your confidence high the first exercise is a two-foot maneuver called double sculling (Illus. 5). Beside taking you across the ice on your own, this will teach you the vital part your knees play in making your skates glide.

Illustration 4

Illustration 5

Stand with your knees straight, heels together but toes turned out so that your feet form a V (5-1). Now bend your knees and allow your feet to slide out diagonally forward, keeping your weight evenly balanced between your feet and on the back center of each skate (5-2). When your skates have slid a few feet apart, straighten your knees and pull your toes together (5-3, 4). As your skates are about to touch, slide them parallel and side by side in a short forward glide before starting the sculling movement all over again (5-5). The scull itself is done on the inside edge of both skates, but be sure you do not "drop" your ankle over to the inside. Only by keeping your ankles firm, will your skates move easily ahead. By repeating these sculls in the same rhythm, you will find you can work up real speed across the ice. Be sure this speed comes from the bending and straightening of the knees and not from the pull of the inner thigh muscles above rigid knees. For the propulsion that comes from the proper use of your knee is the secret of the pushoff onto one skate which is next in the order of learning.

PUSHING OFF

With confidence gained from sculling and baby stepping by yourself, you are ready to try a real stroke. But first it is important to learn the push from standstill (Illus. 6). Place your feet in a perfect T, so that your left foot is behind the right and the heel of your right skate sets into the instep of your left foot at a 90 degree, or right, angle (6-1). Keeping your body upright and your knees straight, put all your weight on your left leg and turn your left ankle strongly in so that the skate is firmly anchored against the ice. Bend both knees deeply. (Illus. 6-1 and photo insert 1). You are now on your mark, ready to go.

Keeping your right foot straight under your upright body, quickly straighten your left knee and at the same instant shift your entire body weight from the left leg to the right (6-2, 3, and photo inserts 2, 3). If you keep your right knee in a deep forward bend, you will find your body is riding easily over a right skate that is gliding equally easily over the ice (6-3).

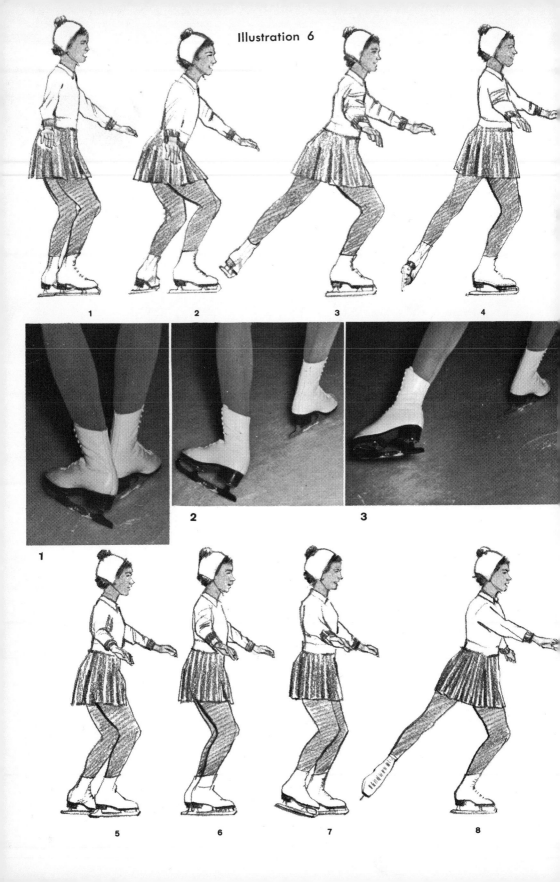

Illustration 6

1   2   3   4

1   2   3

5   6   7   8

Hold this glide as long as you can on a straight line, body perfectly erect and facing straight ahead, left leg fully extended behind, and the left skate only 2 to 4 inches above the ice. I find it easier to balance if I place my left arm forward and concentrate on keeping my shoulders level. Now try exactly the same pushing movement onto the left leg, with the right skate as the T-position anchor. Practice these pushoffs from a standstill many times until you can feel real balance on each skate. Always push from the *flat of the whole blade.* Using your picks for a push from the toe is a cardinal sin of figure skating. The teeth are used only for spinning, jumping, and stopping backward. Play a game with yourself to see how far you can glide from a single push.

From this one exercise it must be clear to you now that momentum *across* the ice comes from the thrust *against* the ice —from the quick straightening of your pushing knee with an instantaneous shift of weight onto the gliding foot. The full power of this thrust (which comes mainly from the muscles just above the knee) is felt when the feet are close together at the moment of weight transference. In this way not only is no energy lost but quicker balance on each stroke is also gained. Experimenting with a speed camera showed that a fine pushoff is made in approximately three-tenths of a second. Beginners, persevere. Experts, check your pushoffs.

Skating terminology

Right here is the place to explain more skating terminology, the everyday jargon of the sport which will become as familiar as your own name after a very few sessions.

The foot that you are skating on is called, logically enough, the "skating" (sometimes the "employed") foot; the foot in the air is called the "free" (or the "unemployed") foot. Dividing the body down the middle, each part of the body that corresponds to the skating foot is called "skating"—thus, the skating arm, skating hip, skating knee, etc. Conversely, each part on the side of the body corresponding to the free foot is called "free"—

thus, the free hand, free toe, free shoulder, etc. In this way a lot of confusing "left," "right" talk is eliminated.

The terms "forward" and "backward," *when applied to the skate itself,* designate the direction in which you are progressing. However, *when applied to a part of the body,* "forward" means corresponding to the front of your body and "backward" means corresponding to the back of your body. Thus if the directions say to hold your free arm forward, or "in front," you are to place it so that the arm carries out the stomach line, no matter whether you are traveling forward or backward. Similarly, if you are told your free leg is backward, or "behind" or "in back," you must place it to the back of your body so that it carries out the spinal line. So remember, front and back position of the arms, head, free leg, etc., have nothing to do with the direction of travel. They merely designate position in relation to the torso of the skater.

Every skating maneuver has three designating terms—namely, the foot you are skating on, the edge the skate is on, and the direction in which you are going—thus, the "left outside forward" edge or the "right inside backward" edge. These edge names are then applied to all the various turns, etc. For the sake of brevity in writing, the abbreviations "L.O.F.," "R.I.B.," etc., are often used. Look around at other skaters and see if you can quickly assign the correct three edge terms to the moves they are making. It will be a help to your own progress if you can gain automatic recognition of all the eight edges—ROF, LOF, RIF, LIF, ROB, LOB, RIB, LIB.

FORWARD STROKING

Now for a fine series of forward strokes in movement (Illus. 6-4, 5, 6, 7, 8). This time, as you make your T-position pushoff onto your right leg, lean your entire body from the edge of your blade to the top of your head in an unbroken line to the right—unbroken, that is, except for the forward bend of the knee and ankle of course. This lean will mean that you are no longer gliding on the flat, or both edges, of your blade but on the outside edge. Keep your free leg extended straight behind, with your free toe turned out and pointed down, until you are ready to stroke left. Then bring the free foot smoothly forward until it is parallel to and touching the skating foot *but not on the ice* (6-6). At this point both knees will again be strongly bent, as the skating knee has kept its initial bend all during the right stroke, and now the free knee must bend alongside it to match it. This will put you in a sort of a squat position that seems awkward in slow motion but in continuous movement is not. At any rate it is essential to a powerful stroke.

Now turn the toe of your right foot out to an approximate 45 degree angle which puts that skate on the inside edge, and simultaneously start your whole body leaning to the left. Without hesitating, straighten your right knee and transfer your weight in the same instant to your left leg and the outside edge of your left skate (6-7-8). The thrust again leaves your pushing (but now free) leg extended straight behind you while your skating knee retains its bend. This completes your stroking cycle: All you have to do is keep going in a steady rhythm from left to right, right to left, etc. As you become more proficient, try lengthening your stroke until you can count at least a slow 1, 2, 3 on each foot. On this plain stroke you should carry your free arm forward, changing arms as you change feet just as you do when you walk down the street. Do not try to lean on an exaggerated curve. This is essentially the racing stroke and should be comparatively shallow.

Remember to turn out the toe of your pushing foot each time, so that the push is made always from the inside edge of your blade, *never* from the toe points. A beautiful stroke is the first essential of fine figure skating, and too much time cannot be spent on its mastery. No matter how facile on your blades you may become, you will never be truly graceful unless you have a straight back, a well-bent skating knee, an extended free leg turned out from the hip, a pointed free toe, an erect head, and relaxed arms, combined with the easy posture true grace demands. This is not a natural position for anyone at first, so you must practice this straight-ahead stroking until you not only feel at home on your skates but are fully conscious of the details of position *as you move* (Illus. 3-B).

By the end of your first half-dozen sessions you should have acquired fair balance and control and should have lost all fear of falling. If you do start to tumble, or if anyone pushes into you, *relax*. Don't stiffen under any circumstances. Sink easily to the ice and you will find it surprisingly soft! Stiffen and you will find it as hard as you have anticipated. My mother, who was skating at least twice weekly at the age of seventy-nine, fell almost every time she skated—to the horror of those who were watching her for the first time. But her companions never worried, for they knew she had been falling as a tumbler falls all her life, in such a relaxed natural manner that she rarely even felt the bump. Don't ever get it into your head that falling on the ice is some sort of disgrace; and don't think for an instant that you will ever become so good that you won't fall. Every skater falls, and this is why it is important to learn to fall without fear, naturally and softly. Right now double up your knees and let your derrière lower onto the ice, as you slide your feet out in front of you. There! It wasn't so bad, was it? Rather fun, really. Remember too that the easiest falls are those taken with speed underfoot, the most painful from a standstill. Accidents to figure skaters, contrary to common opinion, are few and far between.

STOPPING

But stop. Why talk about falls and such? Let's learn to stop effectively instead. The easiest stop—and one you've probably discovered for yourself by now—is the "snow plow." Skate along, slide on both feet, and then turn both toes in (as in the finish of the forward double scull) and skid against your feet, with firm ankles. Be sure to keep your body upright and knees well bent to prevent pitching forward as you come to a dead stop.

Quicker and more efficient is the "hockey stop," which can be done to either the right or the left (Illus. 7). Again skate

Illustration 7

5

9

4

3

8

2

7

6

Illustration 8

1

fast and slide on both feet. To stop left, turn your whole body a quarter-turn left, again bending your knees and keeping your ankles firm. As you skid against your feet (which of course have both turned sideways to the left as your body turned), press your left arm and shoulder hard forward and your right shoulder and arm equally hard back. You should stop short in a few feet by this method. To stop to the right, just reverse all the above directions. T-stops and one-foot stops are good-looking but must be learned later in the figure skating repertoire.

FORWARD CROSS-OVERS

Right now is the time to learn two vital maneuvers—skating backward and crossing-over forward (commonly known as "cutting the corner"). Because you must feel at ease going backward as soon as possible, I want to start you double sculling, and then we'll swing into the forward cross-overs.

The "backward double scull" (Illus. 8-1, 2, 3) is just the reverse of the forward and is actually easier. Place your toes together, heels out in a V, skates on the inside edge but ankles firm. Be sure your body weight is over the balls of your feet, and, of course, bend your knees. Now allow your heels to slide out diagonally backward (as a matter of fact, it was hard to keep them from sliding of their own accord, wasn't it?). When they have glided apart a comfortable distance, pull your heels in together by straightening your knees. Slide with your feet parallel and close for a few feet and then repeat the whole process. It's easy and fun to work up a lot of speed backward this way, so use your knees in rhythm and let yourself go. Two reminders: Never wiggle both feet and your hips from side to side to navigate backward, a common error of beginners, who are often under the delusion that this is skating backward (remember—skating is a one-foot sport), and by the same token, don't allow your feet to slide so far out in the scull that you reach the point of no return!

The cross-overs (Illus. 9) are important to teach you the feel of a very strong body lean to a circle. Properly done, they will strengthen your outside and inside edges in preparation for real figure skating. Carelessly executed, with the sloppy foot movements seen on most ponds and rinks, they will do you as much harm as good. So learn each detail of movement carefully and we'll progress amazingly fast.

To cross-over to the left, or counterclockwise (the easier direction for most right-handed people), stand in T-position

Illustration 9

with your left foot leading, your left arm and shoulder back, and your right arm and shoulder forward. Bend your knees and push strongly onto a LOF stroke, leaving your right leg straight behind, knee and toe extended (9-1). Then bring your right foot forward close past your left (9-2) and cross it wide over in front into the inside of the curve and onto the inside edge of the blade (9-3). As this right skate touches the ice, it should be absolutely parallel to the left skate (toes on an even line), and at the split second of contact all the body weight shifts onto the right leg. This quick shift of weight allows the left skate to *slide* neatly off the ice with the left leg extended, straight-kneed, directly toward the outside of the circle, still in a crossed-under position (9-4). Point your free toe and hold this position while you glide for several counts. Now bring the left skate around close behind the right and touch it to the inside of the right boot in the regular pushing position of a forward stroke. Repeat the stroke and the cross-over alternately around the circle in steady rhythm, working up more speed and a deeper lean. *Do not push* while you are crossing over. Merely glide—every other stroke is a push.

This description of a cross-over is, of course, the ideal that you are to work to attain. I would not expect you to do it like this on your first attempt, or indeed after many attempts. But I feel it is important for you to visualize the desired end result when you start each new move. So concentrate on these points: a body leaning always at the same angle to the center of the circle, a skating knee bent always to the same degree so that there is no unpleasant bobbing motion. This means that your inside shoulder will be always lower and pressed back and that you will push to a bent skating knee and cross over onto an equally bent knee. Only the free knee is straight, and that should be *absolutely straight*. You should feel like an airplane banking around a curve, and the whole action should be as smooth as silk. Try to hold each pushing stroke and each gliding cross-over to an even count of 3. I have a catch phrase which I've found useful in teaching: "Touch—push, 2, 3, cross—wide, 2, 3, touch—push, 2, 3," etc. If you will say this evenly to yourself as you skate, it will not only give you the right rhythm but will remind you of the right movement of the feet. After a few circles around to the left, you must try the cross-overs to the right, or clockwise. Stand in T-position, right foot leading, and reverse all the directions given above. Caution: Do not lean forward from the hips pushing your pelvis back or you may find (like one of our models) that you come a cropper on the picks of your skates. Even if you don't fall, you will look awkward. Do not lean away from the circle at any time. You know what happens if you lean away from the curve while cornering a bicycle? Well, the same thing happens on skates.

Are you having a bit of trouble getting on a really secure outside forward edge? Or a firm-feeling cross-over? It may be that your skating hip is "out," (Illus. 10) and you don't realize it. The most important part of the body in keeping the weight directly over the skating foot is the hip joint and the upper thighbone of the skating side. If, when you bend your skating

Illustration 10

knee, your muscles allow this upper leg to jut out to the side instead of staying in one straight leaning line from your skate, you will never be on true balance, and in extreme cases you will not even be able to strike the correct edge. I always advise beginning pupils to put their own hand on their skating hip joint and upper thigh as they glide over a bent knee to see if they can feel the difference between a pressed in, taut hipline and one that has been allowed to swing out like a hula dancer's. At this point hulas have no place on the ice.

SKATING BACKWARD

While you are working to perfect your cross-overs forward, you must progress from the back sculls to a strong back skating stroke (Illus. 8), preparatory to adding backward cross-overs to the front ones. Surprisingly enough, even advanced skaters often don't know how to stroke evenly backward in a racing stroke around the ice. Crowded rinks make it difficult to practice safely, but pond skaters should have no trouble. In a rink ask a friend to guide you at first until you are secure enough to look around on each stroke. At any rate do not neglect this next important step.

Start with a couple of back sculls (8-1, 2, 3) and, as your feet come together for the glide at the end of the second one (8-3), bend both your knees, then transfer all your weight onto the bent right leg, at the same instant sliding the left skate off the ice in front of you (8-4). Point the toe of this left foot, straightening the knee and making sure the skate is in the air in a direct line in front of the right skate. Do not raise this free skate more than a few inches from the ice! Keeping it low will help to keep your balance forward on the ball of your foot, where it belongs. Any sudden upward jerk of this free leg will tend to pitch you backward toward the back of your head—the one thing we don't want to have happen.

Now bring the left foot back, parallel to the right so that the toe of your left boot touches the toe of your right boot, *but not the ice!* (8-7). Swing your right heel out in a single sculling movement to an approximate 45 degree angle, catching your right inside back edge as you do so; push against the ice by straightening the right knee and at the same split second drop the left skate on the ice directly underneath you (8-8), allowing all your body weight to shift onto it. This quick shift of weight will mean that your right skate will lift from the ice in front and slightly to the side. Move it over directly in line with your left skate, again pointing and turning out the free toe (8-9). The push has automatically straightened the free knee. Leave it that way—until ready for the next stroke.

As you make your next few pushoffs, lean your body to the

side so that you will be stroking each time onto the outside edge. Thus you will realize that skating backward is the same as skating forward, except that all movements are reversed. In other words, we *skate* always on the outside edge, pushing always from the inside edge; we lean the body toward the side of the new outside edge as we catch the inside edge of the pushoff just *before* the new stroke starts; we push and shift weight to the new skate with both feet just as close together and as directly underneath the body as possible; we glide on a bent knee with the body erect above it for accurate balance; the free leg is stretched with toe pointed, whether behind on the forward stroke or in front on the backward stroke; momentum comes from the thrust against the ice gained by the straightening of the bent pushing knee; on all simple stroking the free arm is in front and the arms change as the feet change (as in walking).

Practice this backward stroking until you can "sit" straight down on each new edge comfortably (skating hip pressed hard in and back straight); hold each stroke for at least three slow counts, even longer if you can. But be sure they are even; don't hold on one leg longer than the other or lean more strongly to one side or the other. The ideal is an absolutely even stroke, forward and backward. For proper balance and maximum glide, be sure your body weight is just *back* of the center of your blade whenever you skate forward, just *forward* of the center (on the ball of your foot) whenever you skate backward.

BACKWARD CROSS-OVERS

To cross-over backward (Illus. 11), again reverse all the movements of the forward version, maintaining the same principle of a constant lean to the circle. To cut clockwise, stroke onto a strong LOB (11-1, 2) with free leg well extended in front. Then draw this right leg back and way over in front of the right to the inside of the circle on a strong inside backward edge (11-3, 4). The quick shift of weight will again leave your left foot riding free of the ice, crossed under, and extended straight toward the outside of the circle (11-4). Point the toe and hold. Then neatly bring this free foot around behind the left skate

and touch toes preparatory to the next push (11-1). Again, do
not push on the cross-over itself, alternately push the stroke
and glide the cross-over, *push* and glide the cross-over. The
head looks constantly backward inside the circle. Now turn and
practice the other way. Remember: On all cross-overs, forward
or backward, left or right, the *inside* arm and shoulder are always lower and pressed back, the *outside* arm and shoulder are
always slightly higher and held in front. Look always inside the
circle and in the direction of progress. Throughout, push to a
bent skating knee and cross to an equally bent knee. Don't
rise and bob.

Illustration 11

4   3   2   1

As I intimated in the introduction to this book, there is no
better way of making a stilted, unnatural figure skater than by
letting a beginner advance too soon. The importance of learning to move over the ice with speed, ease, and control before
you start a figure cannot be too much stressed. With justice
modern rink skaters are often called "hothouse skaters" by the
old-timers because they try their figures in a limited space without ever acquiring the graceful easy swing of the great outdoors.
Not that an outdoor style cannot be gained just as well in a
rink; it can, if only beginners, especially adults, will be content
not to rush matters.

Let your children play around on the ice and learn to love
to skate for skating's sake first. The same goes for you. Practice
stroking to music. Hum to yourself if necessary. Hold each

stroke for a full count of 6. Then hold for 12 counts. You will develop a natural rhythm and control that will come in handy later on. Never look at your feet when you skate. Look out and around. Watch where you are going. It's safer—and it also produces better skating posture.

On the theory of one fundamental at a time, we will study the classic edge positions, the four rolls, and the simple basic turns next. Have patience to go along with me slowly now, and not only will you go much faster later on but you will become a far better skater. That I guarantee you.

III

The Four Basic Edge Positions in Eight Classic Spirals

WHEN I use the word "spiral," a new skater immediately visualizes a position with the body bent way forward and the free leg very high in back. That is indeed a spiral position, but it is an arabesque spiral and not the classic variety that I want you to learn at this point in your skating education.

A spiral is neither more nor less than one of the basic four edges skated on either the left or the right foot, held in upright posture with good speed for at least a full circle, and preferably longer. It is called a spiral because if you hold an edge without changing even a fraction the angle of the body lean, the radius of the curve you are making will gradually narrow, or spiral in, as your speed diminishes.

INSIDE FORWARD SPIRAL

The first and easiest spiral to learn is the "inside forward" (Illus. 12). Stand in T-position with your right foot leading. Face your body squarely ahead over your right foot and hold your left arm forward, at the same time pressing your right shoulder and arm back. Your free arm should be held at about waist height, gently curved, and with the hand following out the line of the arm. The palm of the hand should be toward the ice, neither raised from the wrist nor drooped down from it. Likewise the skating arm should be straight behind, palm to the ice. Hold the fingers easily, with the second finger in general somewhat nearer the thumb. These arm and hand directions apply to all edges unless otherwise specified, the forward

Illustration 12

Illustration 13

arm gracefully curved (not bent), the backward arm straight, changing curvature only when they change position.

Without moving your arms at all, take five strong strokes around a circle to the left and hold the fifth, a right inside forward edge. To be able to hold this edge under control for a whole circle, pay particular attention to these points: Keep your hips forward under you and facing squarely ahead, keep your shoulders also at right angles to the line of your skating foot in exact alignment with your hips, and maintain level shoulders with a definite feeling of weight on the skating shoulder. The skating ankle should bend forward (bringing the knee with it, of course), and the free knee likewise should be bent and carried inside the circle almost beside the skating knee. The heel of the free *skate* should be carried directly over the line that your blade is leaving on the ice behind you, but the free *foot,* well turned out and pointed, should be inside the circle. Press the skating hip so hard in toward the center of your body that it feels "hollowed" in. Turning your head over your free shoulder, look to the center of the circle to become conscious of the radius of the curve you are making. Now turn around and follow the same procedure in the opposite direction on the left inside forward spiral.

Are you comfortable? Happy? Or is there a feeling of "pull" as you find your skate spiraling in too fast? One or both of two common errors could cause this. If in the desire to make a deep edge, you lean your upper body into the circle too far, you will take so much of your body weight away from your skate that your skating hip will be out in "right field" and you will lose control of the curve. An even more common fault is a backwhip of the free foot, leg, and hip that will turn your skate sharply into the circle just as a rudder turns a boat. As the centrifugal force of skating this circle makes the free leg *want* to swing out across the print behind, you must exercise constant control through the pelvic area by standing very erect, tightening the buttocks muscles, especially on the free side, and being conscious at all times of the placement of the free foot.

OUTSIDE FORWARD SPIRAL

Next on our list is the outside forward spiral (Illus. 13)—in my opinion, the most important edge in skating. Once you have mastered its sideways body lean, all skating will seem easier to you.

Again stand in T-position, right foot leading so that you will progress around a circle clockwise. Stand with your back to the center of the circle you are about to skate, with your skating hip and shoulder leading and your free hip and shoulder directly behind. Curve your right arm in front of your body, with the right hand a foot or so in front of your stomach toward the outside of the projected circle. Turn your head over your right shoulder. Again without changing position at all, skate five strong strokes, ROF, LIF, ROF, LIF, and hold the fifth on a deep-leaning ROF edge. Lean your whole body to the right from the side of your blade, back straight, hips tight, and eyes turned over the skating shoulder so that you are fully conscious of the angle of lean.

To maintain control, constantly press back your free hip and leg as well as your free shoulder and arm. In this way both your shoulders and your hips will be in line with (or parallel to) the line of the circle (or your skating foot). The free foot, as always well turned out and pointed, should be carried directly over the tracing on the ice behind your skating foot. The free hip, too, should be turned out in its socket so that the inside of the free knee is toward the ice. Contrary to the inside edge position, this free knee should be rigidly straight for maximum control. Your shoulder line should be about level, skating shoulder feeling the weight and perhaps a shade lower. The hips should be definitely level, with downward pressure on the free hip to maintain your balance on the back center of your blade where it belongs. Raising the free hip is a common fault. True, it will press in your skating side and give you a strong feeling of edge but it will, by the same token, pitch you forward and off balance. Keeping the skating hip pressed in is, of course, vital to control, perhaps most of all to this edge, but you must acquire this control through the correct forward position of the pelvis, the tightening of the buttocks, and the strengthening of the upper thigh muscles of the skating leg.

SPREAD EAGLE

To assume an absolutely correct position on this edge requires limber hips. Such limberness is most effectively acquired from diligent practice of a basic free skating move called the spread eagle (Illus. 14). Not only is it beautiful in itself when done easily at high speed and with distinct lean all around the ice surface, but it is fundamental to most skating positions. The ability to turn out the hips, legs, and feet on a 180 degree arc with a lean from the blades in a straight body line makes just

Illustration 14

that much easier all the positions of skating requiring a free leg elegantly turned out from a flat hipline. Many of the school figures, elementary as well as advanced, are easy or hard in direct ratio to the skater's facility in spread-eagling.

At this stage of learning I recommend it to all pupils, adults as well as children. Some find it difficult, some find it not so difficult; most skaters can't fall into a spread eagle immediately and naturally, but for almost no one is it an impossible feat. Although the model for this illustration has now one of the most gravity-defying spread eagles in skating, he was by no means one of the lucky "naturals." It took him five years to acquire the necessary limberness to perform it all ways, to the right and to the left, on the outside edge and on the inside. His facility today has paid him dividends far beyond the effort originally expended. Most adults demur at trying what at first they consider a refined form of torture (one of my protesting pupils even constructed wooden slots to hold his skates out in an arc of more than 180 degrees—a device he named "the torture board"). To doubters I cite my mother, who learned a quite respectable spread eagle in one season at the age of forty-five. My older daughter's partner is another who assured me he had tried for years and would "never" be able to do one; yet at the end of a full season of diligent, *correct* practice, the pair were able to incorporate facing spread eagles into their championship program. Let's hope you are one of the lucky naturals. But if you're not, done with protests, prepare for a few aches and pains now and a lot easier skating later on.

Hold onto the barrier (if at a rink) or a friend's hand (if on a pond) and slide both feet, toes first, out to each side. Press your toes out and around as far as you possibly can at the same time pressing your heels out forward. Keep both knees bent and "drop" both ankles strongly over onto the outside edges until the outsides of the boots touch the ice. Now straighten your knees slowly and pull your derrière up under you. Keep your ankles "dropped" and be sure *not* to arch or pull in your back muscles; this will result in a swayback position that will do you great harm. Just stay as straight as you can and concentrate on the straightness of your knees and the turnout of your toes. Push yourself along the rail, or have a friend push you, until you get the feel of balancing in this position.

The same instructions apply when you try the spread eagle in motion. There are two elementary ways of getting into it. One is to pick up speed, glide on both feet, and then with a sliding motion try to force either your left or right foot (whichever feels easier) in front while your other foot flips quickly, toes out, into a straight line behind it. As your feet slide out, your body must naturally turn sideways. Press your leading shoulder back and let your following arm and shoulder come forward around the curve. You will probably make a straight line at first—or even a reverse curve to the one your skates should be transcribing. Unless you are a natural, you must hold your ankles partially dropped over on the outside to maintain the position, at least until you are limber enough to curve to the outside with speed enough to lean from the edge of the skates.

A more effective method, but one which takes a bit more courage at first, is to skate an outside forward edge on whichever foot you want to lead and then swing the free leg and foot first forward and then back with a vigorous turnout so that it takes the ice behind but slightly *outside* the line of the leading skate. This placement of the trailing foot, especially if the heel is forced as far forward and the toes turned as far back as possible, will *force* the skates to start a proper curve to the outside. Again keep the ankles "dropped" until you have enough speed to lean the whole body to the curve. Be careful not to place your feet too far apart, as this puts undue strain on the knees. Depending on the length of your legs, of course, approximately 2 feet is the right distance between your heels. Pull up on all your muscles, especially those of your abdomen and diaphragm.

Remember: Only with speed can you do the spread eagle correctly with a straight body lean from the edge of the blades, with no break at the ankles or the back. Concentrate on the

Illustration 15

outside spread until you have mastered it. Contrary to popular belief, a *large* inside spread eagle is far more difficult than an outside one; a small inner one does you almost no good as far as limbering goes. Remember, too, that only daily practice maintained off the ice if you can't skate every day will give you the requisite ease. If you skip a practice because you ache, you will only ache worse the next time. A fine spread eagle is not only useful; it is great fun to do and it is an A-1 confidence builder. Once you can lean to its curve, no other lean in skating will give you the slightest qualm.

OUTSIDE BACKWARD SPIRAL

Back to the spirals—backward. Do four or five strong crossovers in a counterclockwise direction and hold the push onto the ROB edge. After a few counts in this plain stroke position, move the free leg, foot, arm, and shoulder backward in a close passing movement, at the same time moving your skating arm and shoulder forward and turning the head outside the circle over the free shoulder. Your hips, which started straight across the line of the skate (with strong forward pressure on the whole free side) should remain in this same position, even though every other part of the body changes. To do this, tighten the buttocks muscles as you move your free leg back and feel as though your free foot, extended and turned out, is pointing toward the outside of the circle behind you. If you curl this free foot back in toward the center of the circle, you will find yourself going into a skid. Be sure to keep your weight on your skating shoulder throughout, with a definite lowering after you have changed into the second position. Raising your skating shoulder and leaning the upper body out of the circle will have the same ill effect of producing an uncontrolled inward spiraling or sideways skid.

Turn and practice this the other way on the LOB (Illus. 15) until you can do both spirals with real speed and lean. If you are young and hope to be a good jumper, this is most important for you, for a majority of jumps land on the OB edge in second position.

INSIDE BACKWARD SPIRAL

Backward cross-overs are again the logical means of getting into the inside back spiral (Illus. 16). After gaining speed moving in a clockwise direction, cross strongly over onto your **RIB** and allow your free leg and foot to move into a leading position on the curve. If you hold your arms and shoulders as previously directed for the cross-overs, you will be all set for the IB spiral, skating shoulder forward and free arm and shoulder pressed back. Both your hips and shoulders should be on the line of the circle so that your stomach faces in toward the center and your back is to the outside, facing just the reverse of the outside forward spiral but with the hips and shoulders in essentially the same alignment—can you see that the difference is merely one of lean and direction? Turn your head over your

Illustration 16

free shoulder inside the circle and watch where you are going. To maintain control, press your free hip constantly backward and stretch your free leg taut. When you are certain of this control through the hips, you may allow your free arm to move forward and the skating arm back, so that the shoulders are gracefully across the line of the skate. Keep looking back over the free shoulder. As always, turn and practice the other way.

INSIDE MOHAWK

While you are perfecting your eight spirals, it's time to learn the first and simplest of the turns from forward to backward. This is the inside forward mohawk (Illus. 17), a turn made from an inside forward edge on one foot to the inside backward edge on the other foot. A mohawk may also be made from outside forward to outside backward, but this is quite difficult to do well and comes at a later stage in your development. If you have practiced your spread eagle diligently, you will find, whether you can yet "spread" easily or not, that the inside mohawk will come off without much effort.

Stand in T-position, right foot leading and right arm and shoulder held forward. Bend and push off on a firm right inside forward edge (17-1), keeping your skating knee well bent and your weight just back of the center of your blade. Press your free arm and shoulder and your free foot back over the line of print. Now, bending the free knee, draw the free foot toward your skate, heel first (17-2). Turn the toes out as much as possible and touch the outside of this free heel to the inside of your skating heel. (You are in effect doing a little bent-kneed inner spread with one foot in the air!—a ludicrous position if held, but quite pleasant as part of a continuous movement.)

To make the turn, reverse the pressure on your shoulder blades, at the same instant allowing your body to turn toward

4   3   2   1

Illustration 17

the left as you shift your weight onto the front of your left skate (17-3) and slide the right one quickly out, toe first, in the direction of travel (17-4). Do not hurry the preparation of the turn—take your time to feel your balance and make each position correct—but once you start to turn, turn like lightning. This is the real secret of success. Once you begin to shift your weight from one foot to the other in skating, or to turn from one edge to another, do not hesitate.

In this mohawk the transition should be smooth but quick, with your free leg, hip, and shoulder pressing back hard as soon as your left skate hits the IB edge. The reversal of the shoulder pressure will thus leave your skating shoulder forward as you ride away backward from the turn. Keep your eyes looking always toward where you are going, that is, the head is turned over the free shoulder after the turn. Maintain a steady lean to the inside of the circle throughout. The skating knee should be flexible, while the free knee and ankle are extended except just before the turn. Follow these directions to the letter and I guarantee you a smooth flowing turn. Lean out, forget to touch your heels, hesitate, forget to reverse your shoulder pressure, stiffen, and you will produce the skids and scrapes that are so common and that ruin so many ice dances. For this turn comes into dance after dance, and for real virtuosity should of course be learned equally well both ways. So turn around and work on the LIF-RIB version.

OUTSIDE FORWARD THREE

Now for a one-foot turn, the outside forward three (Illus. 18 and Illus. 29-1, 2, 3, 4), during which you turn from an outside forward edge to an inside backward edge, rotating in the direction of travel. The pattern your skate leaves on the ice will look remarkably like the numeral 3. This is at once the most famous and infamous turn in skating—famous because it is the essence of the ice waltz, infamous because, when badly learned or learned too soon, it can produce more skids, scrapes, and uncontrolled "whip" than any other figure. Wags have quipped that "only God can make a three," but with detailed understanding of the technique involved and painstaking practice, anyone can cut a fine figure of this turn.

Standing in T-position, right foot leading, place your left arm and shoulder forward, your right arm back. Push off onto a strong *leaning* outside forward edge, back straight, weight on the back center of the blade. With your skating hip held in tight underneath you so that you feel your body weight pressing down through it to your skating ankle and foot, press your free hip and leg back so that they are in line with the circle. If you maintain this hip pressure and *stand erect,* you will find that you can rotate your shoulders against your hips until the shoulder line is approximately square to the skating foot (29-1). With this amount of rotation *plus a strong sideways lean,* very little effort is needed to make the turn. Merely lower your free leg and foot until they are in T-position behind your skate (18-1, 2) and, as you feel your feet touch each other (18-3), shift your weight to the ball of your skating foot and increase the backward pressure on your skating shoulder (29-2). These movements will allow your body to pivot with your skating side as the axis, while the back of your skate lifts from the ice and swings through a 180 degree arc (18-3). As soon as you feel your skate grip the inside backward edge at the apex of the turn, reverse your shoulder pressure and ride away in the position of the IB spiral, free hip and shoulder pressed strongly back, weight on the ball of the foot, and body leaning inward in one straight line. Keep your head facing in the direction of travel (29-3, 4).

Illustration 18

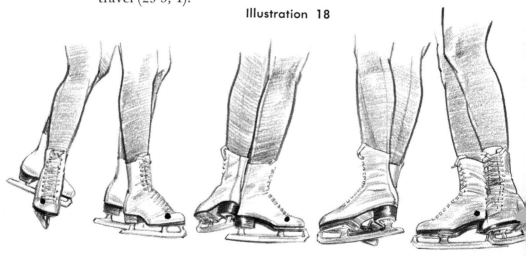

5   4   3   2   1

Controlled use of the skating knee is most important. Push off with a strong forward bend but gradually straighten as you approach the turn. As the feet come together and you start the pivoting action, both knees will be quite straight (18-3). When you feel the IB edge, again bend the skating knee and ankle (without bending at the hips) in a flexible movement that gives a smooth and easy run to the blade. Volumes could be written about this one turn and its uses and abuses. Suffice it to say at this juncture that you must avoid breaking at the hips, either backward or sideways, you must guard against leaning your upper body ahead of your skate, you must not allow your free leg to swing out to the side in a wide arc, and most important of all, you must keep your free hip from rotating forward either before or after the turn. On further analysis, you will see that your lower body does not change position at all from start to finish. You enter the turn with your skating side leading, you pivot completely around and come out backward with your free side leading. Simple, isn't it?

The turn itself must be done, as my first instructor used to say, "in the twinkling of an eye." The cusp of the turn should take no more than 12 to 18 inches of space (depending on the depth of your lean and the size of your foot) and no more than a fraction of a second (18-2, 3, 4). Don't forget to shift weight on your skate. Half the skate must "lift" in any ice turn; a weighted whole blade will always produce a scrape. Keep your skating shoulder a trifle lower throughout, with your body weight constantly on it (29-1, 4).

SOME EXERCISES

As you must realize by now, the same directions keep running through skating instruction. They concern certain body movements that require understanding the muscular action involved. Over my years of teaching I have found that pupils do not automatically know what I mean by what seem to me the simplest directions. For instance, "pressing a shoulder backward" means always to press that shoulder *blade* into the backbone, using the *latissimus dorsi* muscles. It does not mean to exert pressure on the top of the shoulder in any way; in fact, you must be careful not to raise or tighten those muscles, as it will give an unpleasant look of tension to your skating.

If you are finding it difficult to keep a strong forward bend on the skating knee and ankle with an erect body while you stretch the other leg straight, it may be because you have a shortened Achilles tendon. A good exercise to reduce the pull at the back of your heel is this: Stand at the barrier and hold on to it. Lift the toes of your skates against it, with your weight on the points of your heels. Allow your body to bend out back at first, then slowly pull yourself erect, keeping your knees rigidly straight. Gradually decrease the distance of your heels from the wall until the strain is intense. Daily stretching will help a lot. Another useful exercise is to face a barrier with both feet parallel a few inches from it, and then without moving your skates, bend forward until both knees are touching the wall. Make sure your pelvis stays over your feet. Gradually increase the distance of your toes from the barrier. Keep your skates flat on the ice; do not allow the heels to lift. The great Gillis Grafstom, whose footwork was the most sensitive of any skater I've seen, attributed a good deal of his suppleness to daily rotation exercises of the feet inward and outward from the ankle. A word to the wise should suffice.

IV

The Four Rolls—The Waltz Eight

WITH all your spirals and the basic turns under your belt, you are now ready for more formal figure skating, that is, the preliminary figure test and simple free skating. Of course, in a sense the spirals and turns *are* simple free skating. As for the preliminary test, even if you live in an area where there are no accredited United States Figure Skating Association judges to put you through it, I believe you should learn it to regulation test standard, as the control gained thereby will lead you straight into good dancing and better figures. Members of a skating group can test each other, thereby learning the rudiments of judging along with the skating itself.

The four "rolls"—or, as I like to call them, the "half-circle swings"—come first. These consist of semicircles skated first on one foot and then the other, along the same long axis, on the outside forward, inside forward, outside backward, and inside backward edges. You must be prepared to skate at least five rolls on each foot without hesitating or faltering. (The official United States Figure Skating Association rule book calls this "stroking" and does not require the semicircular pattern in the test as long as the edges are true, but most careful teachers insist on the methods I am outlining here, as they lead you painlessly to better understanding and control.)

OUTSIDE FORWARD ROLL

A graphic method is to draw a straight line along the ice with the heel of your blade. Now to do the outside forward roll (Illus. 19), stand in T-position so that the toe of your right skate is touching the line at a right-angle while your left foot is parallel to it. Put your arms, shoulders, and hips in position for the outside forward spiral you have already learned. Push off onto a firm, leaning ROF edge (19-1). After you have held thus (in a position which many skating teachers designate as the number 1 position of the OF edge) for three counts, slowly pass your free foot and leg close forward (19-2) in front of your skating foot and at the same time reverse your arms with a close passing movement. This complete change into the number 2 position should take three more counts, 4, 5, and 6. Maintain your lean to the right throughout (19-3).

As you change your free leg from back to front, allow your skating knee to straighten gradually. As you reach the count of 6, your skate should also have completed a semicircle and be approaching the line on the ice in front of you. Now drop the free foot down beside the skate, parallel and touching in standard pushing position (19-4), and at the same time, bend both knees deeply again. Turn your right foot out a full quarter-turn and push in the number 1 position to the left outside forward edge (19-5), which will again take the ice at a right angle to the line you drew. Repeat all movements, including the rhythmic bending and straightening of your skating knee, on the left edge. Continue right and left all down the ice. Keep counting in slow waltz tempo. Skate your counting. Don't count your skating!

It is important for control that your free hip not rotate forward as you pass your free foot and leg forward—therefore the *close* passing movement that keeps pull to a minimum and allows you to concentrate on maintaining a constant lean. Once you are in the number 2 position, your skating shoulder will be definitely a trifle lower. A second's attention will show you that the number 2 position of the arms and shoulders on one edge is the number 1 position on the next edge. All you have to do at the pushoff each time is bend together, change body lean, shift weight, and turn your head toward the new center. This will be true in general on all the rolls. *And no toe-pushing!* Clean starts from the side of the pushing blade are a "must" on this test.

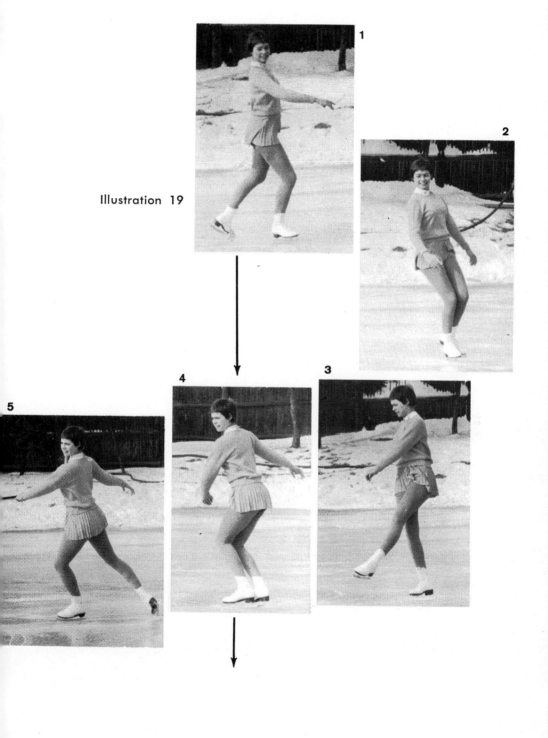

Illustration 19

INSIDE FORWARD ROLL

The inside forward roll (Illus. 20) is started in the same way. Push off into the number 1 position of the RIF spiral (20-1) (most starts in skating are made to the right foot) and reverse your free leg and arms at the halfway mark (20-2) after counting 1, 2, 3, etc. The same bend and rise, the same upright posture. The hips face squarely forward throughout. In the number 2 position (20-3, 5) feel your weight on the skating shoulder, with your skating hip "hollowed" in under you. Also feel as if your free foot is pressing to the outside of the circle in front, while you lean slightly back after it passes; this backward lean is to counterbalance the weight of your free leg in front and should be done on the outside roll as well, to maintain even balance on the back of your blade and prevent any tendency you may have to collapse forward.

OUTSIDE BACKWARD ROLL

The outside backward roll (Illus. 22) is done exactly as you did the OB spiral from the crossover stroke. The only difference is that this time you must start from rest. The standing back starts (Illus. 21) are tricky at first, but if you take care to do the foot movements, the balancing, and the timing as I outline, you will soon have a smooth and powerful pushoff.

Stand so that you are facing down the line you are using as the dividing line for your rolls (21-drawing). Place your right toe on the line and stand firmly on your left skate, which should be parallel to, but 18 to 24 inches to the left of, the line. Place your left arm in front of you and your right out to the side. Now as you draw your right foot over to your left, bend both knees deeply (21-1). Pivot at once to the left on your left skate and, as you do so, start to straighten the knee and push from the inside edge (21-2). As your body completes a quarter-turn in this counterclockwise direction, bring your right foot (which meanwhile has remained still) straight down under you, toe on the line but skate at a right angle to it (21-3). As your right foot hits the ice, transfer all your weight onto it leaning

Illustration 20

hard right. Your left skate, which has by now completed the push, lifts and moves directly on top of the print in front of your skating foot (21-4), just as in your regular back stroke.

Hold this deep back "sitting" position (22-1, 5) (hips square, free arm forward, skating arm back and head looking inside the circle over it) for three counts (22-1), then change position, as for the OB spiral, on the counts of 4, 5, 6. Be particularly careful to maintain your lean to the right as you change position (22-2, 3). By the same token, be careful to change your lean to the left as you bend together and change to the RIB edge of your next pushoff (22-4). In this way you will start the

Illustration 21

left outside edge with your skating hip well in under you and a good lean already established (22-5). *Do not move your head, arms, shoulders except at the halfway point on each semicircle. Pushing should be exclusively from the hips down.*

INSIDE BACKWARD ROLL

The inside backward roll (Illus. 23) has an identical pushoff except that this time you stand with your back to the direction of travel (23-drawing) and you strike a firm inside backward edge right away with your skating toe turned in, as though it were "pigeon-toed." I like to count in a 1-and-2 rhythm all back pushoffs for exact timing of weight transference. Standing at rest is 0; bringing the right foot over to the left and bending together is 1; the start of the pivot and push from the left is "and"; bringing the right foot down and completing the push onto it is 2. This is counted in rhythm as if 1 and 2 are whole notes, with "and" a half note.

As you strike a strong IB edge, your free foot will again be raised, turned out, in front of (but not across) the line of your skate, and your free arm will again be forward with the skating arm held back (23-1). "Hollow" your skating hip way in under you and try to press the hipbone forward toward your stomach as much as possible. After watching your skate take the ice—to make sure it is at a right angle to the dividing line and on a clean inside edge, not a flat or an outside back which slurs over to the inside (judges are very fussy about this)—turn your head over your free shoulder and look back inside the circle toward where you are going (23-2, 5). After the count of 3, pass the free foot so close back that it brushes the inside of your skating foot, and at the same time change your arms (22-2). You are now in the number 2 IB position (22-3, 6), the same as for the IB spiral you have just learned. Your weight, as during the OB roll, should remain on the ball of your skating foot.

For the next pushoff, bring your left toe in to your right toe and turn your left heel out as far as possible. Now holding a firm IB edge, swing your right heel out and push away with a hooking movement (23-4). Watch your left skate strike the new edge. I am a strong advocate of keeping the head and eyes up at all times, but on this particular start, dropping the eyes to watch the new skate take the ice properly is a real help at first. Eventually, of course, you must make a fine start by feeling the direction of your edge while your eyes focus at eye-level, not only for better appearance but for better balance.

You must not expect to be able to make exact half-circles or completely steady edges right away, but with diligent practice of all the movements outlined, I think you will be surprised how soon you will acquire a sense of mastery. The figure eights that follow are just full-circle extensions of these same edges and movements, so every bit of effort put forth now will bring dividends in finer eights very soon. These half-circle swings are the so-called "warm-up" edges used at the start of many club dance sessions. Whether you belong to a club or not, it is wise

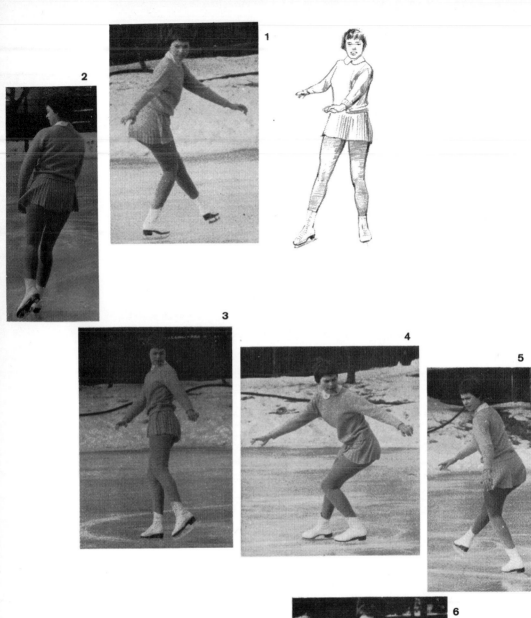

Illustration 22

1

2

3

4

5

6

Illustration 23

to skate them to waltz music as soon as possible. Bring a portable victrola to the ice, or, if all else fails, sing.

WALTZ EIGHT

With the waltz eight (Diagram 1)* you will at last feel that you are really dancing on the ice. This is a figure eight on a fairly large scale with three segments (meaning three pushoffs) to each circle. The first segment consists of an outside forward

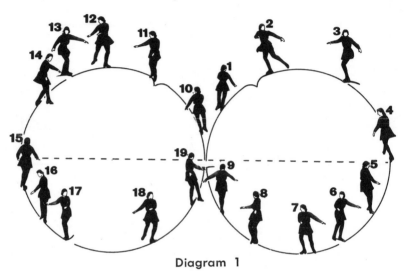

Diagram 1

three, the second of an outside backward roll, the third of an outside forward roll (minus the change of arms). As each segment of the circle takes six beats and the final edge brings you back to your starting place, geometry demands that each part be a third of the circle. The second circle is drawn by doing exactly the same moves starting on the opposite foot. Thus the first circle consists of a ROF three, LOB roll, ROF roll; the second circle consists of a LOF three, ROB roll, and final LOF edge.

Stand in T-position as for the three you have already learned. Trace in your mind's eye the imaginary three-part circle (which you are about to make a reality) right around and back to where

* Numbers in the diagram correspond to the numbers in the related illustration—in this instance Illus. 24.

you are standing. Then look to the other side and do the same. See if you can determine the one-third and two-thirds points on each circle. A strong mental image conceived beforehand will be a powerful help in placing your edges and in making your arms, legs, and torso behave correctly. Imagine a straight line drawn from where you stand to the top of the circle on either side. This will be the "long axis" of your eight and will divide it in half lengthwise. An imaginary line drawn at right angles through the long axis just where you stand is the so-called "transverse" or "short axis" of the figure. Where the two lines cross is where the two circles will meet at the exact center of the diagram, and it is on this center that you place your right toe in T-position. You will create your own short axis by the actual starting edge, while the spot where your edge first shows on the ice will also mark the center of the long axis. In general it takes one skate length to make the edge show from a vigorous pushoff—hence the importance of placing your skating toe on the planned center.

Now (Illus. 24), using all the techniques you have previously learned, push off (24-1) and turn your ROF three on the count of 4 (24-2), holding the RIB edge (24-2) for the counts of 5 and 6. Push (24-3)—without arm or head movement—onto the LOB first position (24-4) and hold this edge all across the top of the circle. Change position as you cross the long axis on the counts of 4, 5, and 6. (24-5, 6) From the finishing LOB spiral position (24-6), let the body turn outward and push onto a ROF edge (24-7) at the two-thirds mark. To make this new type of back-to-front transition easy, bring your free foot, heel first, down *close* to the instep of your skating foot at the finish of the OB edge (24-16, 17) and at the same time allow your skating foot to turn onto a short IB edge (24-6, 7), just as you bend your knees for the pushoff. Make sure your skating hip and shoulder lead all the way back to center on this final OF edge (24-7, 8, 18, 19). To prevent "swing" and also to ensure an easy start for the first three on the next circle, *do not* change your arms and shoulders as you pass your free foot forward on the final 4, 5, 6. Lean strongly to the right until the exact moment you

1 2 3 4

9 8 7 6 5

Illustration 24

turn your right foot to the inside edge for the pushoff to the left three, *after* bending with your feet together. This pushoff should be made right where the first one was—one skate length from the long axis. Again *no* toe pushes. Complete the eight by repeating all movements to the other side (24-10-19).

Always be sure to look ahead to where the next segment of the curve should go. Just before turning your head to the outside of the circle on the OB roll (approximately on the long axis at the top of the circle), take a quick look back down the long axis to the starting center (24-4, 14). As you stroke onto the finishing OF edge, turn your eyes again to the start. Coming back to center is a major judging item. It is wise at first to start from a mark on the ice visible from all parts of the diagram.

This figure is really good fun, especially if you skate it to music with plenty of speed, and lean, and knee bend. Try to

music with plenty of speed, and lean, and knee bend. Try to make it feel like dancing. Your knee should bend and rise and bend again smoothly on each stroke, and your free leg should move in a controlled pendulum motion that looks as graceful as it feels—graceful, that is, provided your free knee is stretched and your toes pointed at all times. Keep your head erect, turning naturally with the movement, and your back straight. One last caution: Be sure to touch your feet before every three and before every pushoff. And pass your free foot close.

Now let yourself go. Right 2, 3, turn, 5, 6; push, 2, 3, change, 5, 6; push, 2, 3, swing, 5, 6; left, 2, 3, turn, 5, 6; etc.—first to the right circle and then to the left.

MAN'S TEN-STEP

Along with the waltz eight—and even before—I always teach the man's ten-step to beginners. This is also part of a bona fide dance, which can be done by couples. However, just for itself it is fun to do alone and has many uses as an introduction to spirals and jumps. So, while you are perfecting all you have learned to date, here is one more item for your fast-building repertoire. I shall merely designate the steps by edge and where the skate takes the ice on each new step. The dance makes a circular pattern, and throughout you lean and turn to the same center.

Start LOF, RIF, LOF, RIF, mohawk to LIB, push to ROB (free foot in front as always), cross the left foot close in behind onto LIB, push to ROB, crossover LIB, and now, bringing your right heel in front of your left heel in a reverse mohawk movement, push onto RIF. If you count each stroke as you make it, you will find there are ten of them. Hence the title. Stretch your free foot back on steps 1, 2, 3, 4, 5, 9, and 10. Stretch it forward on steps 6, 7, and 8. Hold your arms as in the crossovers, the outside arm forward and the inside arm backward, changing position as you make the mohawk and the reverse mohawk. Look always inside the circle in the direction of travel. Simple, isn't it? And fun? Skaters usually feel about now that they are beginning to get some of the icing on the cake of fundamental hard work. Dance the steps, holding each stroke one beat of march time, except steps 3 and 10, which you should hold for two beats each to make the measures come out even. Use the steps in sequences to prepare spirals, for instance, 1, 2, 3, 4, 5, 6, and hold the ROB spiral. Now reverse the whole thing and do a LOB spiral. Hold 9 and turn it into a LIB spiral, etc. The combinations are many and varied. Play around. Make up your own. I want you to feel freedom and confidence on your skates before beginning the study of the two-lobe and three-lobe eights which comprise the all-important school figures of this complex sport. In fact right now you may turn to Chapter VII for the simplest free skating moves and to Chapter VIII for a start on the Dutch waltz.

V

Starting the School Figures

IF you have had sufficient patience to proceed step by step with me to this point, you will, I'm certain, already have mental understanding and bodily control enough to transcribe a moderately accurate forward figure eight right away. As we study the four eights together, you will realize that there are certain fundamental principles basic to all skating. Just as in mathematics, these are axioms that apply to every facet of the sport, free skating and dancing as well as all the figures, advanced as well as elementary. My early years of study under some of the finest instructors in the world combined with my more recent years of teaching thousands of pupils from beginning to Olympic caliber have led me to work out a system of movement in such a way that everything learned at a starting level can be retained and built on right to the Gold Medal or championship level of performance. There are other techniques, other systems that have had signal success; I do not claim superiority for this one. In fact the limberness involved for mastery of this particular technique may make it more difficult at first, but I do feel that, once the fundamental positions are learned, the tremendous control acquired produces better skating faster and easier for a majority of skaters.

So on to the eights, as important to a figure skater as scales to a pianist or *barre* work to a ballet dancer. It is from the eights that all positions and controls necessary to solo free skating, pair skating, and dancing emanate.

My first teacher used to say, "Show me your outside forward eight and I will tell you just how fine a skater you are," and as I have watched skaters over the years since then, I have come to realize ever more strongly the truth of this statement. Hours should be spent acquiring complete control and fine form on this edge; champion or tyro should practice it daily with unremitting attention to detail. Well skated, it is one of the most beautiful of all figures, and every truly great skater works hard to perfect it in his or her own individual style.

Like the larger waltz eight, all eights are so designated because they are formed by two contiguous circles skated from a "center," or starting point, in such a way that they are divided evenly lengthwise by an imaginary straight line called the longitudinal, or long, axis and crosswise by the transverse, or short, axis, an imaginary line drawn at right angles to the long axis at the point where the two circles meet.

The mark that your skate leaves in the ice is called the "tracing" or "print." The tracing itself and the way in which it is made—in other words, the "form" of your bodily movements while you are skating—constitute the two chief criteria of your school figure skating. Every wobble, every sub-curve, every deviation from the true circular edge is a definite fault in a figure. Good school figures are as symmetrical as the native ability of man, unaided by a compass, can make them.

A controlled yet vigorous pushoff, which sends the body correctly onto the line of travel from the very start, is the most important factor in maintaining the one true curve of the circle. As it was for the waltz eight in the preceding chapter, the start of all eights is at the exact center where the long and short axes cross. Stand in T-position with your right toe on the center, your right foot along the short axis, and your left foot, instep to right heel, parallel to the long axis. In other words, your first pushoff mark from this left skate will be one skate length from the exact starting point where your right edge first shows on the ice.

OUTSIDE FORWARD EIGHT, FACTOR 1

Before you start, visualize the circles on both sides of you (Diagram 2). Look along the long axis and determine the top of each lobe. Planning the radius and diameter of both circles ahead of time is a powerful influence in determining the speed and the angle of lean with which you will skate them. (In general the diameter of each circle should be approximately three times your height.)

Now stand in the position of the right outside forward spiral, hips and shoulders on the short axis, with your back to the center of the right circle you are about to skate and with your head turned over your right shoulder, eyes looking in the direction of travel. Be sure you are standing with all your weight on your left leg and with your left ankle turned in for a strong

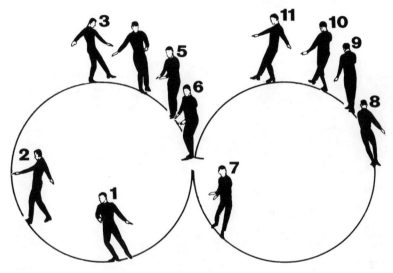

Diagram 2

starting anchor. Now bend both knees and push away from this left skate with a powerful thrust against the ice. Every direction previously given for an accurate pushoff and start should be followed to the letter here.

As your weight shifts to your right leg (Illus. 25), your left skate will automatically rise a few inches from the ice directly over the print. Point your toe and keep this free leg absolutely straight turned out from the hip with the inside of the knee to the ice just as the push left it (25-1). This free leg should remain thus, without any moving or wavering, for the first half-circle (25-2). In fact the whole body, once the initial lean and balance

Illustration 25

3 2 1

4 5 6 7

11 10 9 8

is established, should remain motionless until the skate reaches the point of the long axis opposite the start. I call this the "parallel position," as the skating foot, the hips, and the shoulders form three parallel lines (25-1) directly over the circle but on a sideways lean from it. In this first position, even though the weight is firmly on the skating hip and shoulder, the hip and the shoulderline are level. A definite lowering of the skating shoulder or raising of the free hip will pitch you forward off balance.

At the halfway mark, the skating knee, which of course has remained well bent from the pushoff, gradually begins to straighten, and at the same time you pass your free foot and leg forward and change your arms and shoulders, just as in the OF rolls (25-8). This change into the number 2 position should be complete by the three-quarters circle, and from there, almost to the center, you ride again motionless (25-3, 4, 5, 11). To maintain the weight on the exact same spot back of the center of the blade from start to finish, be sure to lean slightly back to counterbalance the weight of the free leg as it moves forward. Make every movement unhurried and smooth, so that you can keep your body on the exact same lean to the right all the way around. In order to "feel" this lean accurately I pass my arms so close that they actually touch my body and my free foot so close and parallel that it brushes my skating foot (25-8, 9). In the second position the skating shoulder will be definitely lower.

Aside from an unchanging lean and blade balance, the other most important factor in holding a true circle is an unchanging hip position. In other words, on any given circle as the hips start they must finish. They must not be allowed to rotate in the direction of the curve. Hence on this OF eight the free hip is pressed back throughout even though the free leg and foot move forward. To ensure this stability of the free hip it is important to turn out the free foot not only in the back but the instant it passes the skate in front. Only the *heel* of the free *skate* will be on the line of the circle in front. Do not allow the free foot to cross inside the circle either behind in the first position or in front in the second position. The first error will cause your skating hip to jut out, the second will in most cases force your free hip forward and cut in the radius of your circle. Remember: The best skating has the least movement necessary to the desired result.

As you are completing the circle, approximately 2 feet from the start, bring your free foot back beside your skate and at the same time bend both knees preparatory to the next pushoff (25-6). As your skate reaches the first pushoff mark, turn it sideways a full 90 degrees and make a firm instantaneous start from the back of the right skate onto the left outside edge, which should take the ice exactly on top of the original right starting line (25-6). As your right hip leads throughout the right circle and the left hip will lead on the left one, it is vital that the pushing foot turns completely sideways to allow for this full body change at the center. Keep the same speed and the same lean on the left circle as the right and merely transpose all directions to this side. As you ride back to center on the left edge, look at the finishing curve of the right circle opposite. If you have kept an exact lean and balance your left skate will meet this right edge less than a foot from the pushoff marks, just in time for the actual circles to touch before you again turn your skating foot to push off exactly on the same spot. Thus from the place where your circles meet in closing to the place where they separate in starting is, in advanced skating, approximately 2 feet. Beginners are allowed a bit more space, or a wider center of 2½ to 3 feet.

Among the admitted ambiguities of skating language the word "center" ranks high. On this one figure the exact center of the eight is the place where the long and short axes cross, each circle has its own center and the whole diagram is said to have a 2-foot center made by the meeting of the edges before the pushoffs and their separation after the starts. Thus, if you overlap these curves or don't close the circles or start at different points you will be said to have skated a "sloppy center."

Good form in school figure skating consists of upright posture without any bending or breaking at the waist or hips, controlled bend and rise of the skating knee, arms, and hands which are carried at approximately waist height in the easy unstrained positions designated for the spirals, a free foot always turned out and pointed, a free leg under constant control, and a head held erect except for the split second needed to look down at a center or a turn. Anything either stiff or jerky is a fault in style. All the movement should be graceful and even in flow and tempo.

INSIDE FORWARD EIGHT, FACTOR 1

The geometry of this eight and the placing of the pushoffs are exactly the same as for the preceding figure (Diagram 3). The position of the body, however, is diametrically opposite, just as for the IF spiral. Whereas the outside edge starts with hips and shoulders parallel to the skating foot, this edge is skated with hips and shoulders square, or at right angles, to the line of the circle. While standing in T-position for the start (Illus. 26), try to make your hipline as square as possible above your right foot (Diagram 3-1; Illus. 26-1). It is impossible, of course, to put your hips completely on the line of the long axis, but if you will turn your right toe back until it is at an angle of even more than 90 degrees from your left toe, you will find that it helps you to get an accurate short axis start. As soon as you have pushed off, allow your free knee to bend and come inside the circle (26-2, 7) almost beside the skating knee (which is, of course, deeply bent). The free foot, well turned out from the *knee,* will be behind and inside the line of the circle with only the *heel* of the free *skate* over the print (26-7). Hold this pushoff position until the halfway mark (26-3), where you again reverse your arms and move your free foot close forward (26-4) into the number 2 position (26-5, 8) (cf. the IF rolls). Close your circles and push off (26-6) with identical placement, balance, and timing as in the OF eight.

You will find this eight easy and pleasant, and you'll never have any qualms about it. On the other hand, few people do it really well. A fine IF start is difficult to perfect, as there is a distinct tendency to lunge the body forward at the pushoff, and

to lean in too much. It is also much too easy to let the free foot
slip behind across the print to the outside of the circle right
from a vigorous pushoff—a mistake that, just as in your spiral,
will at best narrow the radius of your curve, at worst will cause
your skate to skid. You will find yourself skating a figure six,
not an eight!

The cure for these common errors must be found in an almost exaggerated backward balance on the blade throughout,
which is achieved by holding the hips firmly forward and pull-

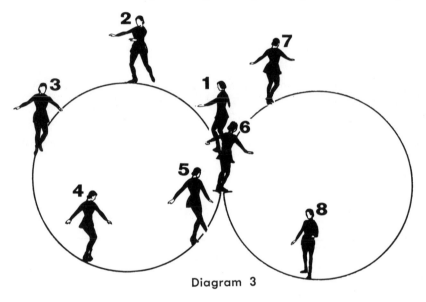

Diagram 3

ing down the base of the spine. As soon as you push, you must
at once tighten the muscles of the derrière, especially on the free
side, and be instantly conscious of the placement of the free
foot. Following the theory that the hips must not be allowed to
rotate in the direction of the curve or change position around
the circle, *forward* pressure must be maintained on the free hip
from the start. Once the free leg passes forward, it is easy to
keep this pressure. It is only the first half-circle that presents a
real problem of control and balance. But if the first half of a
circle is uncontrolled, the second half is always difficult. *It is
the number 1 position of every edge that sets up the eight.*

Because at least three-quarters of the body weight is inside

4   3   2   1

5   6   7   8

Illustration 26

the circumference of the circle, this edge presents a delicate problem in counterbalancing. A strong edge is gained by pressing in the skating hip hard, or "hollowing" it (26-2, 5, 8), and at the same time keeping the weight on the skating shoulder directly over the line of the circle. The shoulders are level throughout. After the free foot passes forward, I have found it helps to press it toward the outside of the circle. As you are closing the circles, look down over your skating side and watch your skating foot meet the opposite circle before you turn it for the pushoff. This is a figure in which it's easy to think the circles have met neatly, only to find on close inspection that the finishes have been diagonal and the starts have overlapped.

The ideal you must strive for in all your figure skating is an even speed. Don't race and don't crawl. One will precipitate you off balance, and the other will give you wobbly lines. Try to finish your figures at exactly the same rate of speed you started them. This can be accomplished only with a judicious bend and rise of the skating knee. (Straightening the bent knee slowly and with muscular force presses the body weight down into the ice and, if the weight is on the right part of the skate, increases the run of the blade.) Don't push any harder, or even as hard, for your second or third circles, as the extra speed will tend to increase their size.

U.S.F.S.A. PRELIMINARY TEST

At this point you can, if you are so inclined, take the official United States Figure Skating Association preliminary test. You have all the technique necessary. Even if you don't live where accredited judges are available, it is well, as I said earlier, to get friends with sufficient knowledge to give you a judging once-over. In a sport as exacting as this, to meet a definite standard at the start is a real help.

The test consists of the four rolls, the waltz eight, and the outside and inside forward figure eights. It is not difficult to pass. Judges do not demand perfectly controlled edges at this stage of skating, but they will expect you to look as if you know what it's all about—that is, starts on the correct edge, no toe pushes, an approximation of accurate pattern, and in the three eights a definite ability to come back to the same starting point each time. On the waltz eight the three turns must not be scraped or jumped, a certain amount of symmetry is expected, and each stroke must come reasonably close to lasting the same amount of time and covering the same amount of ice. Skate ten rolls on each edge and three eight circles on each foot and each edge. The waltz pattern is repeated three times to each side. The repetition diagrams should trace the original one with moderate accuracy.

In judging the preliminary tests no marks are assigned to the rolls. The judges merely write "pass" or "fail" according to the accuracy of these steps. If a roll is judged a failure the test automatically stops right there; if all the rolls pass the eights come next.

Each eight is assigned a mark from 1 to 6. The mark 1 designates a very badly skated eight, 2 equals faulty, 3 means passing, 4 equals good, 5 is excellent, and 6 perfect (hence, 6 is seldom if ever given). One-tenth marks in decimal points can and should be used to designate further intermediary values, for instance: 2.8, 3.5, 4.2, etc.

Each school figure has also acquired a factor of difficulty over the years. The factor ranges from 1 for the most elementary figures to 5 for the most difficult figures in the Gold Medal category. The mark assigned a figure in a test must be multiplied by the factor for that particular figure. As the factor for the preliminary test figures is obviously 1, merely add the total of marks given the three eights. If they total 10.2, you pass, provided no figure gets below 3.0.

OUTSIDE BACKWARD EIGHT, FACTOR 1

Depending on how well and confidently you have learned to skate your back rolls you will find this eight either very difficult or just moderately so. At any rate, getting the requisite power and balance at the start to carry you evenly around a full circle will take a bit of practice. Diligent application toward perfecting now the technique of the pushoff and start will pay you dividends for all your skating life and will make the complex backward figures later on much more fun.

The timing of the pushoff I described for the rolls (Illus. 21) should be practiced as a separate exercise. Draw a cross, representing the long and short axis, on the ice with the heel of your blade (Diagram 4). Now stand and count start after start until you can place your skating foot on the short axis line exactly at the cross time after time. Make a game of it. Practice from right to left, too, as a few figures from now you will need a powerful standing start in this direction also. During all the movements of the standing pushoff, keep both feet in your line of vision and make sure that you actually *see* your skating foot take the ice each time. It's easy to think that you have pivoted sufficiently, only to find that you haven't kept your skating toe turned in and have at the last split second put it down too soon, resulting in a hooked start on the ice.

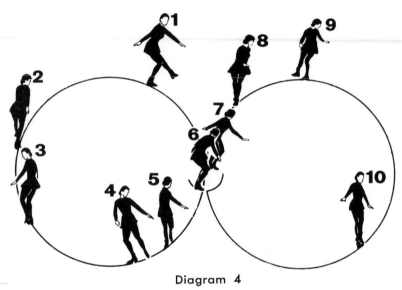

Diagram 4

Try for as little arm movement as possible, so that as your body starts backward along the short axis, your shoulders are already in place along the line of the circle, skating shoulder pressed well back and free arm and shoulder pressed forward, matching the pressure on the free leg and hip. The balance of this start is tricky, and it takes a lot of concentration for a skater to be able to *feel* whether he is pitched slightly backward ahead of the blade or is truly balanced on the ball of the foot leaning only to the center of the circle (Illus. 27-1). Though eventually you must be able to turn your head over the skating shoulder at once and look inside toward the quarter-circle mark, it is useful at first to practice looking only at the center of each circle as you ride in the number 1 position up to the long axis; in fact, practice holding this first position all the way around a full circle. If you can do this, you'll have few, if any, problems with this eight.

The skating ankle remains bent way forward so that the knee is beyond the point of the toe for the first half-circle. It is a true "sitting" position. As one of my instructors used to say, "Imagine you are sitting in a straightbacked, old-fashioned chair—and then someone tipped the chair to one side"—a pretty good description. The skating hip is pressed hard in, and the line of the hips is strongly square. The free thigh should close in over the skating thigh (27-1) as soon as the pushing foot completes the pushoff and lifts from the ice. The knees should never touch, but you should feel as if your pelvic area is one solid block.

When you change position (27-2) between the half- and three-quarters circle as usual (27-4), you must make certain that the outward rotation of the upper body (27-2, 3) and the backward movement of the free foot does not include the hips. In order to keep them stationary and the pressure on the free hip constantly forward, tighten the buttocks muscles as you pass the free foot back, and feel as if this foot, well turned out, is pointing to the outside of the rink or pond. Never let the free foot curl around behind you or your curve will curl correspondingly.

In order to feel the same angle of lean all the way, I always pass my arms and free foot as close as possible (27-3). From level shoulders during the first half-circle, you will have a definitely lowered skating shoulder in the second position (27-5). Look back down the long axis to your starting point at the half-circle (27-2) and then out to the three-quarters mark before you turn your head around. The head may move quickly on the neck, but the shoulders must rotate slowly. Once turned, look along your free side for the opposite circle and your closing center, but do not commit the common error of dropping your free shoulder down and your head and upper body outside the circle in a misguided effort to watch your lines. Dropping the

Illustration 27

3   2   1

4   5   6   7

8   9   10

free shoulder will shift your weight to the back of your skate and cut in your curve. Leaning out will widen the radius and cause you to miss your center.

The real secret of success on this eight is a supple waist. If you stop to analyze the fact that during one half-circle the upper body must be twisted against the rotation of the circle, and during the other half it rotates the other way—all without disturbing the lower body or changing the lean—you begin to realize that limberness is of the essence. Twisting exercises off the ice will be very valuable about now.

As you close your circles and bring your feet side by side (27-6, 7), with bent knees for your pushoff, be sure to start your body lean toward the new circle as you change edge for the push from the IB edge (27-6). This does not mean that you take your weight off your pushing foot; it merely means that changing lean on the pushoff itself will ensure a solid start with the new skating hip well in underneath you (27-8), provided, of course, you do not reach out with the skating foot before you transfer your weight to it. Move only the pushing foot; keep the other one motionless over the short axis on each start, ready to receive your weight (26-7). For the hairline accuracy needed here, it is necessary to look right down at your skates, but if you are on the proper lean, this is only a matter of dropping the *eyes* straight down. Do not move the arms or the head or the hips on these pushoffs. Push from a square position on one foot to a square position on the other straight along the short axis. Because it takes a little more space to push backward than forward, diagram centers on the back eights may be a little wider than 2 feet.

FORWARD CHANGE OF EDGE

ROIF-LIOF and LOIF-RIOF, Factor 1

This figure, far less difficult for the beginner than the preceding one, is merely a combination of the first two edges you learned, namely the outside forward and the inside forward. It is made in the form of a three-lobe eight (see Diagram 5). "Change of edge" means that at the halfway mark of the first circle (d3) you come up on the flat of your skate from your right outside forward edge and then shift to the right inside forward edge (d4), starting a new circle which you then hold steadily back to the point where you made the change of edge. Here you push off on the left inside forward (d6) for a half-circle, completing the circle of the middle lobe as you reach your original starting point where, instead of stopping, you come again onto the flat (d9) and change edge to the left outside forward (d10). This you hold around a full circle to finish out the end lobe (d11, 12), coming back once more to your original start. Both changes of edge cut the long axis at right angles.

Thus you see that the middle lobe is comprised of half an outside circle on the right foot for one side and half an inside circle on the left foot for the other. This means that in order to do both changes of edge (that is, from outside to inside and

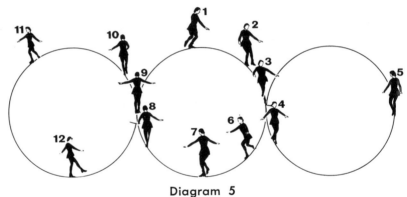

Diagram 5

from inside to outside, on both feet) you will have to make another whole diagram, starting with the left outside forward changing to left inside, and completing the figure with the right inside changing to right outside. Many of the combination figures from now on will have to be started first to the right and then to the left in two separate diagrams in order to ensure that all the changes and all turns are made on both feet. The instructions I give will be only for the first diagram, starting right, and will merely have to be transposed and repeated for the same figure started to the left.

Stand as you would for an outside forward eight pushoff with

your hips on the line of the short axis, but this time ease your
shoulders around until they are almost square to your right
skate. Look up along the long axis and decide just where you
are going to make your change of edge, and then carefully
plan your *three* circles accordingly—before you start. On a
three-lobe figure it is particularly important that you judge
your space and examine the quality of all the ice you are going
to cover ahead of time.

After the pushoff hold a deep knee bend and a motionless
position until the quarter-circle (Illus. 28-1); at this point start
a slow upward pressure of the skating knee and an equally slow
forward movement of the free leg and the skating shoulder
(28-2, 3). Make sure you keep a strong inward lean to the center
of this half-circle all during the passing movements (28-3), which
should be timed so exactly that your free leg reaches its maximum forward swing right at the point of the long axis. When
the free foot thus is at the apex of the half-circle, move it
quickly back so that, as your skating foot reaches the long axis,
the free foot is brushing past it in a backward movement. At
this exact split second change your edge to the inside forward
(28-4) by first bringing your body up straight into "neutral"
and then over to the new circle with another strong knee bend
and a "hollowed" skating hip. As your skate catches the inside
edge, change your shoulders to the standard inside forward
eight position and make sure your hips are also square. Take
care that, with the added momentum of the change, your free
foot does not swing back across the print behind, but takes its
correct place just *inside* the circle. Complete this IF circle back
to the change center just as in the plain eight (28-5).

As your skate closes in to the change of edge line, push in
standard LIF position (28-6), making sure that your left skate
takes the ice exactly on the change. Look up at once to your
original start and, again from the quarter-circle, time a passing
movement of the free leg and a straightening of the skating
knee to this exact point (28-7, 8). Allow your free arm and
shoulder to press gradually more forward as you draw toward
your change, and this time, as you make the change (28-9) onto

1   2   3   4   5

9   8   7   6

Illustration 28

10   11   12

the LOF edge with a decided lean of the body to the left, leave
your shoulders just as they are with the left shoulder of course
lower (28-10). Meanwhile your free foot has passed back close
and quickly as it reaches the long axis (28-9) and your free hip
has pressed back with it, so that as your skate grips the OF edge,
the hips are parallel, the shoulders square (28-10, 11). Complete
the OF circle back to place without further movement of the
arms but with the usual passing movement of the free leg
(28-12), observing all the previous rules for skating this edge.

On analyzing the description above, you will realize that the
actual lower body position changes as your skate changes edge
and you enter a new circle with a new rotation. This change of
position can only be effected through the free side of the body,
as one of the cardinal rules of skating says that the *skating hip
must remain pressed in and completely motionless at all times.*
To change pressure on the free hip from forward in the square
position of the IF edges to backward in the parallel position of
the OF edges requires definite limberness. That is why I insist
upon practice of the spread eagle and other stretching exercises.

The change of edge itself occurs in the space of approximately
half the length of your skate, as your skate shows two edges, or
a flat, on the ice for a few inches while it is changing lean from
one edge to the other. This flat place should occur right at the
top of a true half-circle without any bulging or flattening of the
edge before it. An improper S change is produced by the first
error, a diagonal change by the second. Rotating the hips along
the half-circle, leaning in too much, or jutting out the skating
hip are the common reasons for an S change; changing body
lean to the new circle before the long axis is reached results in
a diagonal line. Smooth movement of the free leg and exact
timing of the change itself are the absolute essentials of a fine
serpentine figure. As for the forward eights, the entire space of
transition between circles should be only 2 feet on an expert
figure. A little more leeway is allowed beginners.

The three circles should be perfectly evenly laid along the
same long axis. In order to ensure equal size and uniformity of
side line of the three circles, you must always look ahead to the

key points—that is, the change point from each start, and the quarter-circle, the half-circle, and the three-quarters circle in that order around the end lobes. As you pass the halfway mark on each end circle, be sure that you raise your eyes to check that the sides of your three circles are all in a straight line. From the three-quarters mark I always look over to the quarter mark of the next center lobe before looking back to the change point to watch the circle closing.

There! I have given you in a few pages the accumulated lore of my skating life, on these figures. I can only say that too much emphasis cannot be put on the acquisition of a refined change of edge technique.

Changes forward or backward are an integral part of a large number of figures in the skating curriculum and they are the essence of every one of the Gold Medal figures. Properly done, they impart a lovely rhythm to school figure skating; due to the rise and bend of the skating knee they help maintain an even flow throughout the circles.

Because it is admittedly easier to control the hips above a stiff skating knee, changes have all too often been taught that way, with very restricted movement of the free leg and without the free flowing use of the skating knee which in my opinion, because it is the essence of beauty in free skating, should be learned and faithfully practiced in figures. The official rules require it, but rules are all too often bypassed, even by the officials who create them. If this particular rule were insisted upon in test and competition skating, there would be more great school skating and less boredom with figures among our young skaters all over the world. Stiff skating is dull, and a stiff slow figure is no fun for either the skater or the onlooker. A beautiful flowing school figure can be just as pleasing to watch as a fine free skating program, as the great school skaters of the world, from Gillis Grafstrom to the present, have proved. Rhythmic figures in turn produce more truly rhythmic free skating.

Of course jerky or off-time movements will raise even more havoc with serpentine figures than stiff restricted ones. There must be no compromise with the split second timing and real muscle control that are needed to skate a successful change by the methods described above. Swinging too soon or too late, using the knee spasmodically, bending from the waist or from the hips so that the upper body anticipates either the pushoff or the change, all are mistakes guaranteed to ruin your diagram. So stand erect, pass your free foot always close with an exact turnout before and after, move your arms easily, and have fun with rhythmic changes. Skating them to waltz music or to your own counting will give automatically good timing. Try counting three slow beats per quarter-circle of skating and see how well it works. You will find all your major movements start on a strong beat—1-6 for the starts to the change, 1-6 from the change to the top of the end circles, 6 more back to center. If your speed diminishes, of course it will take a few more beats for the end lobes, but try to achieve the even speed and lovely rhythm of the steady count.

THREES-TO-CENTER

RFO-LFO, Factor 1

I consider this one of the most important figures of all. In my early competitive days it was in the international schedule (in fact, I made my international debut at the Winter Olympic Games of 1928 in St. Moritz, Switzerland, by literally falling flat on my face through the soft ice while skating it for the judges!), and I sometimes feel our competitors today would achieve a higher average of school skating if they had to keep it in practice beyond the first test level.

The control, limberness, and quick balance that it takes to place these forward turns on the apex of two true circles, with an almost 180 degree turnout during the IB to OF transition from one foot to the other at the center (Diagram 6-5, 6, 7), are a fine *barre* lesson in themselves. The incomparable Tenley Albright, during the years she was winning her world and Olympic titles, practiced this figure almost daily.

Each three is skated exactly as described earlier, and if you have learned to do your waltz eight with real control, the

greater control needed to place the turn on the half-circle mark
and hold the IB edge steadily back to center should not prove
too difficult. Remember to rotate your shoulders against your
hips from the pushoff to the turn. That means a free shoulder
forward against a free hip that is pressed constantly back and
a skating shoulder blade drawn back into your backbone while
your skating hip is under you forward and leading (Illus. 29-1,
2). (A word of caution here: A skating hip is said to be forward
merely because the other hip is backward in line behind it. Do

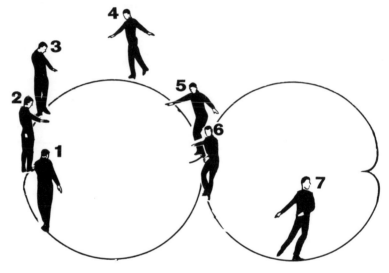

Diagram 6

not make the mistake of thrusting the hip *out* forward any
more than you would let it jut out sideways.)

Free leg and skating knee action is even more important here
than on the waltz eight. Let your well-bent knee rise slowly
from the quarter mark to the turn. *Just* before going into the
turn itself, close your free leg, straight-kneed and turned out,
in behind your skating leg with your feet in complete T-position (29-2, 3 and 18-1, 2, 3). As you shift your weight from the
back center to the ball of your foot and tighten the skating
shoulder blade a fraction more to motivate the pivot of the
turn, be sure that you keep your feet touching (18-3). As you
feel your skate come through the turn onto the IB edge, re-

Illustration 29

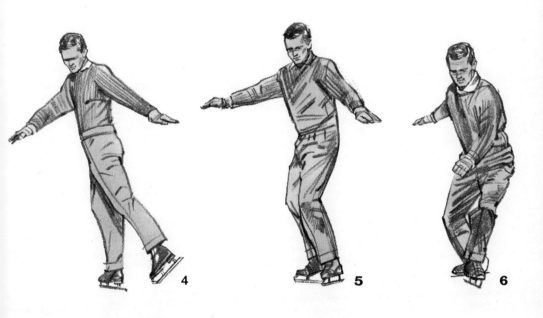

1 2 3

4 5 6

verse your shoulders, bend your knee again, and let your free foot and leg stretch out, straight and pointed right along the path of the rest of the projected circle (29-4). All this movement is so quick (about $\frac{3}{10}$ of a second) that when I do my best threes, onlookers often don't realize that I have touched my feet at all, let alone kept them touching throughout the whole cusp of the turn.

The control of the IB edge all the way back to the starting center is achieved by what is technically known as "checking." "Check" here has the meaning of the word "stop," and to check means to stop rotation by reversing the shoulders. In other words, by pressing the free shoulder back as you come through the point of the turn, you help to hold the backward pressure on the free hip also, thus stopping the rotation worked up by the shoulders versus hips "torque" before the turn (29-3, 4). The skating shoulder meanwhile, slightly lower and with the weight on it (to maintain the balance on the ball of the skating foot), moves forward to keep the body in one straight, leaning, unrotated line (29-3, 4, 5). The only movement from the turn to the center is a gradual upward pressure of the skating knee again.

As your skate nears the start, bend both knees deeply and at the same time bring in your free leg and foot so well turned out that the free heel can rest against the inside of the skating heel (29-5). As your heels touch, start your body lean toward the new circle and at the same instant turn your skating heel out so that you make a clean push from the IB edge straight onto the OF edge (29-6). (This pushoff mark will leave a tiny "tail" on the ice toward the new circle.)

Complete the three on the corresponding circle with the movements described above. The only difference will be an inability (at least until you are expert) to rotate the shoulders immediately after the transition from back to front. However, you must rotate them fully as soon as you can, at least by the quarter-circle. Remember: Not one bit of this technique will work the desired result on the ice unless you *stand erect* at all times, with a straight back and the muscles at the base of your spine pulled down and tightened throughout the entire diagram. You must *feel* the point at which rotation of the shoulders against the hips must stop. If you break forward at all, your shoulders will go right on turning with nothing to stop them, until your body weight is way ahead of your skate and your turn is ruined.

What is the desired result on the ice? Round circles and steady edges with the three turns placed exactly at the top of each circle facing straight down the long axis to the center. The two halves of each circle and the two halves of each turn cusp should be so symmetrical that if you cut the figure in two, lengthwise, and lapped it over at the long axis, one half would match the other exactly.

Over and above these generalities true to all figures, the turns must be "clean." This means that the skate must make the transition from the OF edge to the IB edge right at the exact point of the turn. As you practice, take time out to examine your threes closely—on your hands and knees looking against the light if need be. Two lines on the ice are the telltale signs of a flat, or a change of edge, which mean that your skate came up straight and shifted edges either too soon or too late. The flat that shows on the ice is often called a "double edge." If you have perfect balance the shift from one edge to the other will occur right at the point of the turn, leaving a minute open space. An "open-top" three is the ideal for which you must strive. There should be no thickening or gouging of the edge before or after the turn, the quality of the tracing should be the same on both sides, and on the top of your turn there should be no toe mark (known as a "spoon") from the teeth of your blades. The turn, in other words, should be the natural result of the lean and twist of your body and should not be forced through the ankle. Judges see so few of these easy unforced threes in advanced skating that when they do see them, they often forget to give the large extra credit such fine balance should earn.

A good tip for accurate placing of your turns is to look on each pushoff at the point on the long axis opposite your starting toe where you intend to turn—and don't take your eye from that spot until your skate reaches it. Your skating toe, incidentally, should feel as if it were pressing out of the circle right from the start until the split second that your skating side turns down the long axis. Another word of caution: Be sure that at the center you keep your feet very close together while pushing from IB to OF. A wide step will almost invariably mean that your skating hip will be thrown out on the OF edge, and you will not be able to recover perfect balance to start your twist on time.

And what is the best exercise to aid in turning perfect threes? The spread eagle, of course.

UNITED STATES FIGURE SKATING ASSOCIATION FIRST TEST

Having learned your figures thoroughly thus far, you are ready for another test of your ability. The preliminary test is a useful starter, but it is with the first test that the United States Figure Skating Association gets down to the serious business of determining how good a skater you are. There will be seven more of these proficiency examinations until the eighth, or Gold Medal, test is passed. If you can possibly do so, join the association through one of its approximately 500 member clubs all over this country and Canada. If there is no club near you, independent memberships making you eligible for tests, etc., in any skating center are available for a nominal sum. However, if you are so situated that this seems a useless procedure, give yourself the test. It will be useful, and also fun, for you to evaluate your practice so far according to the judging rules that will follow.

Use as clean and unmarked a piece of ice as possible, so that you will be able to see your tracings clearly. If more than one of you are taking the test, skate each figure in rotation and then go on to the next. For example, in this first test all skate the OF eight, then the IF eight, the OB eight, the forward change of edge starting right, the same serpentine starting left, and finally the OF threes-to-center. Start each figure on the right foot just as you have in practice (first indicating with your arms the long axis to be skated), then retrace each lobe twice on each foot, making three prints in all. It is best always to place your figures either lengthwise or crosswise on the ice surface—in practice as well as during a test. When you have finished, examine the figure carefully, looking for all the technical points your instruction has stressed so far. In evaluating a figure, the print on the ice counts first, then the form in which it was skated (here it is difficult to judge yourself!), the size of the diagram, and finally the closeness of the repeating lines.

Now mark the figure on a scale of 1 to 6, according to how good or bad it seems to you. For non-circles or wobbly edges deduct a lot; for open-top threes or changes on the top of true half-circles, add a bit as a plus for special virtue. Since all the first test figures have a factor of 1 merely total your marks and see if you have equaled the passing score of 21.6. If you have, you've passed providing no single figure received less than the passing mark of 3. A failing mark for any one figure in a test means failure, no matter how good your other figures may have been.

You passed? Great! You are entitled to a real sense of achievement. You failed? Don't be discouraged, but practice some more before you go on to the next figures. Many a champion has failed the first test he or she ever took—as I did. True, you may never want to take this test officially, but mentally you must take it. If you are satisfied with your progress so far, give yourself the fun and relaxation you have earned by starting to learn all but the most difficult dances and all the free skating your present ability will allow. I hope you have not been so unwise as to have gone beyond the most elementary dances before this point. I am a strong believer in walking before running, and the fact that a majority of dancers never become really good dancers is due to an early neglect of fundamental edge control.

One more series of figures to go (those in the United States Figure Skating Association second test and the next chapter) and then you will be a solidly grounded skater, ready to go on to any goals you may have set for yourself.

VI

Completing the Fundamental Figures

INSIDE BACKWARD EIGHT

RBI-LBI, Factor 2

The very fact that this eight has a factor of 2 indicates that the authorities consider it a more difficult edge to form into matching contiguous circles than the preceding three. It is—and no doubt about it. The difficulty lies primarily in achieving a powerful, accurate start and a firm finishing curve that closes in to the center without straightening, sub-curving, or changing edge before the pushoff (Diagram 7).

As for the corresponding roll, you stand with your back to the first circle at the pushoff. Now with the bend-together, pivot, and push rhythm you have already learned, thrust powerfully away from your left skate, consciously using the leg muscles above your left knee. As you pivot a quarter-turn left, allow the right side of your body to come as far forward over the short axis line as possible. You should feel your skating hip "hollowed" hard in toward your stomach the split second your right foot makes contact with the IB edge. If you make this pivoting movement accurately, you will be able to turn your body so far that, as your left skate rises from the ice at the finish of the pushoff, your free hip will be able to relax back in such a fashion that it is actually leading on the line of the circle. The pushoff mark itself will be a curlicue, often called a "rat's tail," which should end approximately at the long axis. "Dragging" this pushoff line is not only a fault of print but it actually means that your body weight and body position are not accurately placed over your skating foot as the edge starts.

The arms and shoulders meanwhile, after a slight movement to the left (Illus. 30-1) as your feet close in for the pushoff, move to the right so that at the moment of contact they are on the line of the edge, skating shoulder pressed back and free shoulder forward (30-2, 3). The shoulder line is level with the weight on the skating shoulder. The head also turns to the right (30-3), enabling you to watch first your start and then a few feet of the arc of the circle. When this is well done, you will feel that the heel of your right foot has swung way out to catch the edge

Diagram 7

straight on the short axis while your toes turn in. In fact, the whole body position of the start is hard for a beginner to understand. Nothing seems to look the way it is. I like to explain it as a "kitty-corner" position. The skating hip is forward and the skating shoulder back; the free shoulder is forward and the free hip is back as far as is physically possible, with the free leg in front and the shoulders in a rotating position. To maintain a firm edge with no tendency to rotate the hips on the first half-circle, it is necessary to bend the ankle hard forward right from the start (30-3), with the trunk of the body in a straight forward sitting posture, while the thigh of the free leg closes in to the thigh of the skating leg (30-3) and the whole free leg turns out from the hip, straight of knee and pointed of toe. Great care must be exercised that this free hip does not "drop" and that

Illustration 30

3   2   1

4   5   6   7

the free leg does not swing out into the circle, thereby pulling your weight off your skating hip. Conversely, the free foot must not be allowed to swing across the print in front to the outside of the circle, thus causing uncontrollable rotation of the hips.

After riding a few feet in the starting position, turn your head over your free shoulder back inside the curve (30-6) so that your eyes can look up to the top of the circle at the long axis. This is the one eight where I permit movement of the body before the halfway mark. Some skaters find it easier to let the free shoulder start back and the skating shoulder forward before the free leg commences passing. It also seems to help occasionally to let the skating knee begin to rise at about the one-third mark. But by no means should any movement (except the head's) start before this. Firm control of the first half of the circle is, as always, the secret of a controlled finish, even more so on this eight than any other.

Once at the apex of the curve, move the free foot so close back that it scrapes past the heel of your skating foot (30-4) and continues straight along the projected line of the rest of the circle (30-5, 7). After the leg is at full extension, turn it out from the hip again and make sure you maintain an even backward pressure. Pointing your free toe hard helps you to be constantly conscious of this pressure. Keep your back straight and tighten your buttocks so that you feel your body in one leaning line to the center of the circle with your skating shoulder lower and your weight as always on the ball of your foot (30-5, 7). (Try putting your free foot down in an inside spread eagle at the three-quarters mark. It's a good exercise.)

Now have the patience to hold this completely parallel position without moving until your whole skating foot closes in onto the short axis opposite your pushoff mark. At this point bend your knees again and bring your free foot in. As the heel of your skate rides past your original pushoff mark, "drop" the skating ankle way over to the inside and, with the weight on the ball of the skating foot, at the same instant swing your heel out in a forced-edge hooking movement from which you may produce another powerful thrust. This pushoff requires one of the few forced edges in skating. Meanwhile the free toe has come in to touch the pushing toe just before the hook begins. With heel pressed out as far as possible in this pigeon-toed fashion, you begin the new edge cleanly right on top of the first one. Scraping the starts or slurring over from an outside edge to the inside edge are considered major errors on one side of the center, just as are sprawling flattened lines which trail off into a formless finish on the other side. To close in properly and thrust cleanly with real power takes fine timing, which is acquired only by a lot of diligent practice. Even after competing for years, I used to spend a few minutes practicing this eight for speed and power almost daily.

As with all eights, the finishing position on one foot is the starting position of the other foot, so try to move your arms and shoulders as little as possible on each pushoff while concentrating on bending your knees and turning your lower body only. Just as with the outside forward eight, a complete change of body position occurs with each new thrust. If you can actually turn so that your free hip is leading at the start of each circle, you will find that if you shift your weight completely, you cannot "drag" your pushoff lines—your pushing foot *has* to lift from the ice.

Before even trying the backward change of edge or the outside-forward-inside backward threes, it is imperative that you have the inside backward eights under real control. (Many teachers believe that this edge comes too late in the curriculum and should be taught along with the outside backward eight. No harm will be done by starting it earlier.) So while you are practicing faithfully, we will go on to turns that do not involve this edge.

INSIDE FORWARD—OUTSIDE BACKWARD THREES

RIF-LOB and LIF-ROB, Factor 1

In general outline, this figure is the same as threes-to-center —that is, a three turn facing straight down the long axis occurs at the apex of each circle. I feel the inside forward three is the easiest turn in skating—it practically makes itself—but the outside backward turn presents a few interesting problems of rotation control in both the upper and lower body (Diagram 8).

Pushoff on the RIF with the skating shoulder forward and the free shoulder blade drawn into your backbone (Illus. 31-1). This is the position you have been using for your inside mohawk, not the position of the spiral where, of course, the free shoulder is forward. In other words, it should be clear by now that, as a fairly general rule in skating, when you want to turn

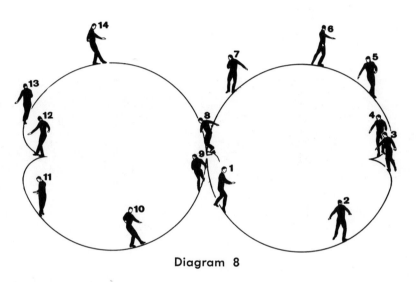

Diagram 8

your body around toward the center of the circle, you twist your shoulders in the rotation of the circle against your hips; when you want to maintain an edge without turning, you hold your shoulders against the rotation of the circle. (An exception, however, is the starting position of the inside backward eight!)

Observe all the regular rules for square hips, straight back, free foot inside the circle, etc., of the IF eight and keep a steady shoulder pressure right to the turn (Illus. 31-1, 2, 3). I find the best balance when I have the skating shoulder just slightly higher in a sort of "banking" position on the curve (31-2). As this right shoulder leads you into the three, you are going to shift your weight from the back center to the ball of the foot

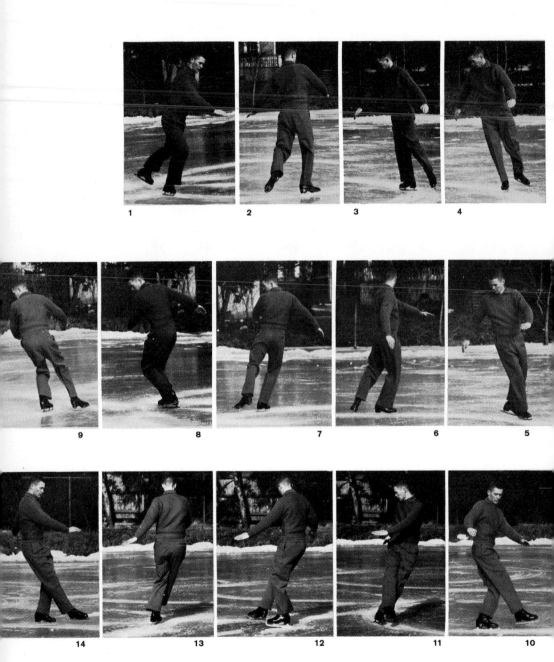

Illustration 31

and turn naturally onto your right outside backward edge (31-4). If you have started off with a strong inward lean, you hardly need any extra tightening of the left shoulder to motivate the turn. Some skaters lower the free foot to the heel of the skating foot with good results, but I prefer to keep my free foot perfectly still and just turn around (31-4). My free foot thus moves from slightly inside the circle before the turn to slightly outside the circle after it (31-5). As always, the turn itself is lightning fast.

As your skate feels the OB edge, reverse your shoulders and look in toward the three-quarters mark (also take a quick peek back to your start from here) (31-5). Once at the three-quarter, turn your head to the outside but do not change your shoulders (31-6). Hold thus to your center (31-7) and push off to LOB with your shoulders still in this reverse position (31-8). Keep the skating shoulder lower on the OB edge out of the forward turn and the weight steadily on it until you make the back push (31-5, 6, 7, 8).

After this reverse-shoulder back pushoff (31-8, 9) (which may seem strange at first, but after a few times will feel quite natural), look in toward the quarter-circle mark for a few feet (31-9) while you are consolidating a strong square body position; then turn your head to the outside of the circle as the whole upper body twists around for the turn (31-10, 11). Remember that this twist is *against* the hips, while the body lean remains always strongly to the center of the circle and the weight is on the ball of the skating foot (31-11). It stands to reason that to keep the weight thus, you must keep your skating shoulder lower with your weight firmly on it. Rotation pressure is, of course, on the free shoulder blade which is drawn firmly to the backbone (31-11).

The crux of control lies in getting the free leg in firm position as soon as it lifts from the pushoff (31-10). Place it immediately over the print (turned out so that the tracing shows under the arch of your foot); squeeze the upper thighs together but make sure that your knees do not touch (31-11). Keep a strong constant forward pressure on the whole free hip and leg so

that as your upper body rotates to the outside, your free leg
will not fly out of the circle (31-11), thereby ruining control of
the curve before the turn and the turn itself.

The only movement from the quarter-circle to the turn
should be the gradual straightening of the skating knee (31-
10, 11). The straightening pressure here is particularly useful
in helping hold out the curve of the circle. At the point of the
long axis, repeat the usual weight-shifting and shoulder-tight-
ening as, without any other movement, your whole body turns
quickly toward the center of the circle (31-12). Bend your knee
and reverse your shoulders as you feel your skate on the new
IF edge (31-13). Ride back to your start in this completely
checked position, with your body sideways to the center of the
circle and your skating hip strongly "hollowed" under you
(31-14). (Throughout this entire circle and turn I like to feel
that my lower body is one solid block, first traveling backward
and then traveling forward.) On the theory that the least movement necessary produces the best results, I do not move my free
leg or foot for either three. However, if closing in for a turn
produces less disturbance of the hips, then do it by all means.

This method that I have finally adopted as the most satisfactory after years of experimentation with many other techniques
means that there is only one shoulder change per circle—that
is, the checking movement after each turn. Placing the forward
three is easy (look at the long axis opposite the pushoff and
keep looking at it), but placing the backward three presents a
new problem. This is essentially a "blind" turn, and you must,
in the final analysis, *feel* when your skate has reached the top
of the curve. However, planning the whole diagram ahead and
looking at the long axis at the moment of the back start (31-9)
and again giving it a quick glance just before turning the head
to the outside will help. Do not make the mistake of trying so
frantically to see that you lean out of the circle (if you lean
strongly *in,* you will see more easily). Remember that here, just
as in the IB eight, the head turns on the *neck* and can make a
quick revolving movement without disturbing the shoulders or
the upper body at all. (When I watch some of my pupils, I am

wont to ask them if they turn their heads with their stomachs! Test yourself on any back circle and see if you can turn your head first one way and then the other without moving your shoulders at all—another useful co-ordination exercise).

Presupposing that by this time you have your backward inside eight in satisfactory shape, we will now proceed with the study of the all-important backward serpentine.

BACKWARD CHANGE OF EDGE

ROIB-LIOB and LOIB-RIOB, Factor 2

This figure's formation is identical to that of the forward serpentine, except that where the outside and inside edges were

Diagram 9

forward there, they are backward here. The placing is the same (Diagram 9). Again let me warn you not to attempt it unless your two backward eights are really secure; if you have the slightest doubt, go back and take one more lick at the back edges by themselves. The combination figure is admittedly difficult at this stage of skating, so don't hurry on to it. A hasty start now will mean much wasted effort later on.

If you feel confident of your control, make the ROB pushoff (Illus. 32) exactly as for the ROB eight and hold this first position for a quarter-circle without movement (32-1). Now pass your free leg back in a steady, smooth "draw" that finds your free foot brushing your skate on its way backward (32-2, 3). Turn in this free foot slightly and watch inside the curve for

1

2

3

12

11

10

Illustration 32

4

5

6

9

8

7

it to reach the long axis (32-3) (the point where you have been looking since the start). At this juncture quickly move the free foot close forward (32-4) and change to the inside backward edge. Timed exactly, your two feet will be opposite each other at the split second of changing (32-4).

Note that there is no shoulder movement whatsoever throughout this first half-circle, and there will be almost none during the next half-circle. The change should be so quiet as to be hardly felt. From a strong lean to center on the OB edge (32-1, 2, 3) it is a matter of leveling off with even shoulders and a "hollowed" hip as the new circle is started (32-5). The IB circle is completed just as in the corresponding eight (32-6).

At the change center push to LIB with vigor. After watching your skate hit the middle of the change line and travel on a firm curve a few feet farther (32-7), turn your head (without disturbing the rest of your body—remember?) and look for your original pushoff mark. Slightly before the quarter-circle reverse your shoulders and pass your free foot close back (32-8) in movements identical to those for the IB eight change-of-position, so that you are looking along the curve in a firmly parallel position as you near your first start.

When you see your free foot reach this starting edge, pass it quickly forward (32-9) and sink into a deep, "sitting" outside backward position identical to that used before the OB three (32-10). Make certain you keep your body weight on your skating shoulder both entering and leaving the change center (32-8, 9, 10); a drop of the free shoulder here can pitch you backward with disastrous results. Maintain this strong rotated shoulders versus square hip position for the first half of the OB circle, sitting balanced over the ball of the foot on a well-bent knee (32-11). From the half to the three-quarter circle, move the free foot slowly and closely back (32-12), making sure you tighten the buttocks to keep the necessary forward pressure on the free hip to maintain a square position as the free leg passes back. Hold this second position and close the circles just as in the plain OB eight.

All the general rules for smooth skating of the entire diagram may be transferred from the forward serpentine. The knee action is similar throughout. Looking from one radius to the next radius beyond the long axis to make sure you hold your curves out after each change, looking along the entire sideline from each end lobe to check the line-up, and sighting the long axis for the exact timing of each change, are all even more important here. It is easy to cut in one lobe, especially the OB.

Once you are set to change edge, make the transition quickly. A hesitation will give you an unsteady line between the two circles and an unfirm position on the new edge. This does not mean rush; it merely means to move with precision. As you come through each change, think of keeping the skating hip firmly in under you. From the OB to the IB edge, think first of pulling down on the base of the spine and tighten both buttocks as you pass your free leg back (32-2, 3), then consciously relax the free hip as you strike the IB edge (32-5). From the IB to the OB edge you must have constant pressure on the free leg and hip, first back along the curve before the change (32-8), then hard forward as the free foot passes at the long axis (32-10). Any mistiming here, especially of the body lean to the new circle, will result in a weak, wandering, uncomfortable position which I call "no man's land." It is one of the worst sensations in school skating; if you feel it, make sure you are keeping your skating side firmly in under you while you lean decisively from the center to the end circle, and check the timing of your free leg. There is very little sensation of changing from outside to inside; there is a lot from inside to outside. After this latter change, due to your lean your free hip will *look* higher because of its square position, but actually you must neither raise nor lower it inside your body. Remember: One of the tenets of my system (contrary to much teaching) is that the hips are always level.

One more three turn to learn and we will have completed the foundation of our skating structure. Be sure to spend equal practice time on your left foot diagram; if you have worked on your standing start from right to left, as recommended earlier, you will be all set in both directions.

Many skaters become so intrigued trying to perfect the right foot figures during a given practice session that they forget to go on to the left foot diagram—and the next time they repeat the process. These are the ones who become "right-foot skaters," and you must make sure you are not among their number.

OUTSIDE FORWARD—INSIDE BACKWARD THREES

ROF-LIB and LOF-RIB, Factor 2

The eight is formed by a plain forward three for the first circle and a reversal of the forward turn (that is, a three turned from the inside back edge onto the outside forward edge, in the direction of rotation) for the second circle. This means that, just as in threes-to-center, you are going to make a regular ROF three to RIB which you hold back to center (Diagram 10-5); then instead of making that complete outward rotation of the free hip onto the LOF which you found difficult in your first test diagram, you are going to turn out your left *heel* and pigeon-toe for a push directly onto your LIB, as in the IB eight.

However, this time you are going to keep your head looking out to the left and your shoulders rotating for the full half-circle before the three (Illus. 33-1, 2). In this position the great difficulty is not to rotate the upper body (and, with it, the hips) too far. You also have to guard against a natural tendency to lean backward. Either error will ruin your control of the turn or the circle, or both. I like to call this the "position of equilibrium" and often liken it to a pair of old-fashioned grocer's scales. Your weight should be evenly distributed throughout the trunk of your body between your skating hip and your free shoulder in such a way that you feel your balance through your skating hip and leg down to the ball of your skating foot (33-2). To achieve this delicate balance, raise your skating arm so that you can look *over* your hip and *under* your arm (33-1). (One of my instructors used to say, "Feel as if your skating hand is resting on the top of a table.") (33-1) Be sure your shoulder line remains level, however, as a raised skating shoulder will mean too much inward lean with a skating hip jutting out; a lowered one will mean a backward pitch with serious loss of balance.

As always on a back inside start, compress the skating hip hard in and relax the free hip back (33-1, 2). I find it useful to toe in the free foot slightly on this ride to the three turn (33-2), as it seems to "lock" the hips in position and allow a more controlled rotation of the shoulders against them. In any case, pigeon-toed or straight, be sure that this free foot does not cross over the line of print to the outside of the circle. Press up the skating knee slowly from the quarter mark to the long axis (33-2, 3), at which

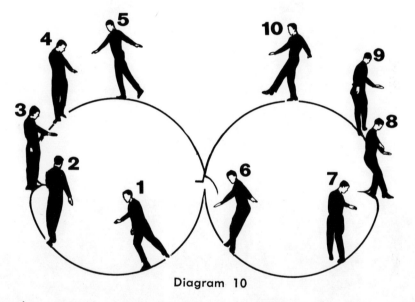

Diagram 10

point you again shift weight to the back center of the skate and turn around (33-3, 4). Let your head go around the turn, and as soon as you feel the OF edge, check your shoulders (33-4). Now look over your skating shoulder back to the starting center (33-5). Maintain a strong sideways lean all the way "home," with a definite feeling that your skating side is leading along the curve, with your free shoulder pressed firmly back (33-4, 5). To keep the free hip back without any desire to rotate forward and curl you in, turn out your free foot as soon as you turn (33-4).

With this figure the curriculum of the second United States

Illustration 33

1

2

3

4

5

Figure Skating Association test is completed. If you give your-self the test, assign a mark to each diagram as before, but this time multiply by 2 as well as 1, according to the factor of each figure. The passing total is 43.2, with a minimum of 3 for any one figure. If you skated a perfect test (no one ever has), your score would be 72.

BASIC THEORY

Now seems a logical time to review the basic theory, those axioms of technique, which I mentioned earlier. You have enough mastery of the four eights, the two serpentines, and the four three turns to realize that certain principles run through all the figures studied so far. Those same principles will apply to all your future skating, no matter how advanced it may be-come or how elaborate some of the turns and movements:

1. The weight of the body must be as much as possible over the skating foot.

2. The skating hip must be pressed in toward the center of the body and held motionless at all times.

3. The hips must not be allowed to rotate in the direction of the circle rotation. To effect this, since the skating hip is im-mobile, muscular pressure must be exerted through the pelvic area in general and the free side of the body in particular to counteract and control the natural desire of the lower body to turn with the circle.

This means specifically that, in the system of skating deline-ated here, the free hip is pressed back on the OF and IB edges (hips in line with skate in "parallel" position as much as pos-sible); on the IF and OB edges the pressure on the free hip is forward (hips at a 90 degree angle to the line of the skate, with the free hip inside the circumference of the circle on the IF, outside the circumference on the OB). These positions will en-sure that the skating hip is constantly being pressed against the rotation of the circle that is being skated.

4. The lean of the body is always to the center of the circle from the side of the blade.

5. The body weight rides on the back center of the blade on

forward edges, on the ball of the skating foot on backward edges.

As a corollary to rule 5—the body weight must never travel out ahead of the skate either forward or backward.

6. The hips remain level inside the body.

7. The skating knee is in general flexible and "working." Pressing the knee slowly up (hence, the weight down) increases the run of the blade.

8. For all three turns, the shoulders rotate against the hips beforehand, the body leans strongly to the circle center, and the weight shifts from back to front of the skate for a forward turn, from front to back for a backward one. The turn is a quick pivot of the whole body with the skating side as the pivoting axis, made not by a conscious effort of the foot but by the twist, or "torque," of the body before the turn.

As you continue practicing, it becomes increasingly important for you to pay strict attention to the matching size of your circles, to maintaining an absolutely straight long axis for each diagram, and to the close retracing of your lines. The general shape of the figure—that is, the evenness of its lobes and the placing according to axis—must be attended to during the first tracing. If this tracing is accurate, you have merely to worry about putting the next lines on top of the first. Do not make the common mistake of trying to "steer" your skate around the retracing diagrams. This is the cause of more bad school figures than any other. *Skate* your repetition figures. Skate them the same as the first figure each time. In other words, *repeat* your lean and your movements and your timing exactly.

A useful hint is this: It is easier to retrace with a good eye if you always make your first circles as large as you want the finished figure to be and then aim to place the retracing lines just inside the original tracing. In this way you always have a line to aim for and run less danger of wandering far afield from your first diagram.

Another useful hint: In practice never retrace an incorrect print. This does you more harm than good. Make sure your original figure is correct first, and then retrace. When skating before judges, for whatever purpose, it is better to correct a first tracing error in the second tracing and then place the third over the second than it is to retrace an incorrect line closely each time. If you correct an error and then retrace the corrected line, it shows that you know what is right and *can* do it. You will get more credit than for closely traced incorrect lines. Good judges demonstrate that they judge this way over and over again, but it is hard for a teacher to convince pupils that they do. Slavish retracing of faults is the worst tendency in modern figure skating. It is up to all judges and all officials to demonstrate by their judging at all times all over the world that correct print and good style are the most important factors in good school figures.

From here on in you can dance or free skate like mad. You have all the basic control needed for either or both. Remember the same edge principles apply, whether you are jumping or dancing the blues. Just as all work and no play makes Jack a dull boy, so all school figures and no free skating will make you a dull skater. (After all, it's because you really want to dance and free skate that you've spent the time mastering the edges, isn't it?) There is an endless amount of fun in store for you. But don't go overboard. Whether or not you learn more figures and go on with tests and competitions (in which case you must keep up with your figures), these basic figures should always be part of your schedule. *They* are always the ultimate test of your control.

VII

Free Skating

How to tell you how to free skate? That is something I'm afraid the written word cannot completely accomplish. Written instruction can teach you much and help you greatly, it is true, but after a while precept and example plus your own native ingenuity will be necessary. A thorough treatise on free skating, even for beginners at the art, could easily occupy a whole volume by itself, while many wonderful free skating moves cannot be written down, for the simple reason that they have not yet been invented.

No one person could hope to make a compilation of all the dance steps and varied free moves that have already been skated, and no one imagination could envision all the possible new combinations. That is the fascination of skating. "Time cannot wither nor custom stale her infinite variety"—so with pure figure skating, there is always something more to learn about its siren charms. If you haven't yet made that discovery for yourself, I guarantee that you will after a few weeks of experimenting with the spirals, steps, jumps, and spins that follow.

As in all your skating so far, you should learn your free skating in its natural sequence. If you are young and ambitious, don't try jumps before you can control the spirals described in Chapter III. Don't spend hours trying to spin like a top without devoting an equal amount of time to learning how to weave steps into dances. Don't try a complicated jump before you can do the simplest ones in good take-off and landing position with steady edges and controlled balance throughout.

If you are a dancer, don't try to interpret music on ice before you know the correct skating means for such interpretation. (This goes for free skaters as well.) There is nothing more

Illustration 34

B

A

ridiculous than a skater who tries to gain an artistic effect that is beyond his present powers. Don't think that because you like to fling yourself about with speed and abandon, anyone else will like to see you do it. Speed and abandon, yes, but with grace, style, accurate footwork, and control over all your moves. Above all, learn how to *glide* from one figure to the next. You should practice your plain stroking, your cross-overs, and your rolls as warm-up exercises every time you go on the ice to free skate or dance. They should be standard procedure for acquiring that effortless "flow" over the ice surface that is the mark of the fine skater. Even an untutored audience at an average show is quick to sense that a skater who doesn't have this quality is not really a good skater, no matter how spectacular certain of his specialties may be.

If you are no longer as young as you once were or if, perhaps, you are a naturally retiring person who would feel self-conscious trying solo free skating moves, my advice is the same —only different! You don't have to fling yourself about at top speed, you don't have to spin at all, you don't have to do even one jump to have a tremendous amount of fun with your free skating and to become a very pleasing performer. You will combine spirals and dance steps in interesting patterns, skating always in perfect rhythm with the music. You will be able to skate well with others in carnival groups, and eventually you will be doing all sorts of things you probably don't think possible now.

You will gradually lose your fear of leaving the ice, and you will try the easiest of the jumps. You will find that you can do them, too (there are many skaters who have learned the simple jumps when they were well beyond the half-century mark!), and, surprisingly enough, spinning is easy. Once you get the knack of rotating on one spot (and if you'll think about it while you learn, that isn't very hard), there is nothing to basic spinning except standing still and going around! So abandon your inhibitions and come join our free skating class.

Free skating is the icing of the cake. It is exhilarating exercise and grand fun. There is one point to get well in mind before we start: It is not *what* you do, but *how* you do it that counts. My first instructor used to say that to me on the average of once a lesson, and I still think it the best advice.

BASIC SPIRALS

As I pointed out back in Chapter III, the spirals you were learning are the classic edge positions, extended in a large curve. Everyone can do them, and they are not only great fun for the skater but, when done with speed, freedom and real style, are beautiful to watch. These same spirals may be done with a change of edge, so that you are covering a large amount of ice surface with your original momentum. You may change from OF to IF, or from IF to OF, swinging your free leg first forward and then back, just as in the corresponding school figure. You may also—and with good effect—change from IF to OF without moving your free leg at all, except to press it harder and farther back as you come through the change. This is a little more difficult than the other method but worth perfecting, for a change spiral done like this—from the landing of a half-flip or a split jump, with the body going over into an arabesque position after the change to OF—is a good move, requiring real control.

The change-edge spirals may also be done backward in a variety of ways. For instance, after stroking forward to gain speed, do the first six steps of the man's ten-step on a large curve and hold the regular OB spiral position (second position of the eight) for a half-circle or so. As you cross the long axis of the ice surface, change edge to the IB, moving the free foot forward but without changing the arms or head. After riding like this about a quarter-circle, pass the free leg back again and reverse the arms, with the head still over the free shoulder looking back where you are going (a very necessary precaution in a crowded rink, and one too many skaters forget! Most skating positions are designed to allow the skater to see those around him—if he will just look. Not looking is the most common cause of accidents, so train the eyes now). This spiral may also be done by reversing the arms at the change without moving the free leg.

A good-looking change spiral uses this same reverse IB

position (free leg back, free shoulder forward) on the first half (do the six-step preparation, plus a deep crossover) and then draws and drops over to a deep OB, with a sharp change of body lean and a complete reversal of arms and free leg at the transition, as in the regular inside to outside backward school figure change. This is an athletic move and must be timed with precise and decisive movement to make it work. If you are a female, try leaning the upper body backward after the change, raising the skating arm over your head, pressing the free leg hard forward and quite high, with your head turned back over the free shoulder. This latter position, done to extreme, can be spectacular (but take it easy at first—it requires real balance). As you must have gathered by now, there are myriad variations of arm and leg positions. Try everything you can think of, and be sure to try them on both feet. My pet aversion is the advanced skater who comes to me for a free skating lesson and says, "Oh, but I can't do a good inside forward spiral on my left foot. I can only do it on my right!"

If you are a male, don't think spirals are just for girls. The great Gillis Grafstom made his famous IF spiral a specialty. He did a deep-leaning IF edge with *both* arms and shoulders *and* his free leg pressed hard back; then at the depth of the curve he gave a quick knee bend and straightened instantly into a very erect straight OF done on the diagonal with skating arm and shoulder forward, free arm and leg and hip back, head turned forward over his skating shoulder in classic pose— a most effective move which, done with Grafstom's feeling for line and style, never failed to win applause. Hayes Alan Jenkins, in his Olympic routine, so excelled in another variation of the IF spiral that it almost became his trademark. Hayes, with free arm way forward, allowed his free leg to swing back across and outside the curve behind his skating leg, as he bent deeply on a terrific edge. As I'm sure you realize, only great muscular control and a skating hip compressed hard under him would allow him to hold such a basically unorthodox position. In pair skating it is essential that the man as well as the woman be able to do fine spirals. Yet most of the pairs that have come to me for training in recent years have taken more time to unify their spirals (with the man the culprit) than any other aspect of the program.

As I said earlier, "spiral" in common usage always brings to mind a position where the body of the skater is way forward, the free leg very high behind, and the head up with a strongly arched back. This arabesque position of the body is extremely important and may be incorporated with all the changes of edge and turns to produce an almost infinite number of spiral variations. The arabesque position is also used in spinning by both men and women, alone as well as combined with jump spins. So it is important to learn to do it well as soon as your edge control allows.

Skated in correct form, an arabesque spiral is a thing of grace and beauty. Done badly, with a humped back, a bent free leg, an unpointed free toe, a drooping head, angular arms, or any other ungainly body position, and it at once becomes ludicrous. A good arabesque requires limberness; if you are not limber to start with, stretch until you are. Stretching will make you feel good—after the first few days! You will discover muscles, tendons, etc., you didn't know you owned.

I think the best way to learn the basic arabesque position is first at the barrier and next on the flat of the blade in a straight line down the ice. It is wise to have a friend watch you, particularly at first, as it is difficult to *feel*, especially if you are at all stiff, whether everything is in its proper place. Stand facing the barrier with the free arm and hand crossed under the skating arm on the rail. Raise the free leg—straight, turned out, and the toe pointed—as high as you can with your body erect and your hips *level*. This will not be very high perforce. Now, without lifting the free hip or the free side in any way or breaking the line of the body at all, rock your body forward at the skating hip as far as you can. If you keep your head up and your back arched with a strong pull on all the muscles, your free leg will automatically rise as the trunk of your body gradually creates an arc. If tightened "hamstrings" behind the knees don't prevent a full stretch, your free foot and your head will be the even ends of the arc. Eventually your free foot will go even higher. As you stretch, be careful to keep forward and downward pressure on both the free hip and the free shoulder. The whole trunk of the body should be as horizontal to the ice as possible. It is as if your body were a seesaw, with your straight skating leg its fulcrum.

Once you have a moderately good arabesque at the rail (be sure to do it on both feet), try it gliding straight down the ice. Start in the same way and rock your body over, holding both arms easily out to the side so that you form a perfect horizontal T. When your audience approves of this moving position—first on one foot, then the other—try leaning to all the edges, forward and back (Illus. 35), left and right. Again there is a great variety of possible arm and head positions. One of the best known is the "Bror Meyer spiral," named for one of the famous teachers of the sport, who invented it. (Many figures in skating are similarly named after their first exponents.) Lean in arabesque position to the OF edge and allow your free arm and shoulder to reach way forward, while pressing the skating arm and shoulder back. To make the body line a curved sideways arc from free hand to free toe, you must bring your free arm in a curve close to your ear. (It feels *too* far forward when it's right.) Turn your head to the inside of the circle. Well done, this is a very graceful, leaning pose.

No spiral, however, is first-class unless it is absolutely steady. The free leg should rise into place in one motion and must remain there, unwavering, for the duration. "Moving statues," someone has called spirals, and that is an apt description. The arms and head may change, and for that matter, the trunk of the body may change from upright to arabesque or vice versa, but each position in itself must be firm.

Pivots

Having whizzed down the ice and brought off a good spiral, you must now have an ending for it. A common and effective finishing move is the pivot. For many years pivots were neglected by young skaters, but luckily they are now back in favor, thanks to the Jenkins brothers, though not in the profusion or fancy varieties of my father's day. Pivots should never go out of style, for they lend interest and grace to programs for both men and women. In pair skating, a controlled OB pivot is a "must" for any man who expects to take his partner successfully through a "death spiral" (Illus. 36). (I suspect this maneuver got its name when a skater who couldn't pivot properly sent his partner crashing onto the back of her head!)

Pivots are really not a bit difficult and should be learned by every beginning free skater. As the OB is the most common, we will start with that. In England it used to be called a "curtsy," which gives you an idea of its effect. (This name should not deter men, for on ice it is a thoroughly masculine move.)

Most of us find it easier to start a pivot from a right edge, turning around to the left; so from whatever spiral you are on, maneuver (if forward, turn a three, etc.) onto your ROB. Wait until your speed diminishes, as it is difficult to learn a pivot from a fast wide-angle curve, though eventually, of course, you will swing into one that way. Bending both your knees deeply, swing your free foot way around straight in back of your skating foot toward the absolute center of the curve. Jab its toe point firmly—and straight down—into the ice, at the same time turning your right heel consciously out a bit (See Illus. 36). Shift most of your body weight to the toe-point leg and pull back hard with this left shoulder, turning your head to the left, too. This means that your right skate (with any weight you have on it on the ball of the foot) will be pulled in a small back circle all the way around your left toe point. You should keep your body erect with arms out; your bent knees and the position of your feet give the curtsy effect.

After a turn or so like this, pull your right foot in, straighten your knees, and come to a stop with both feet together. If you have your body weight distributed as directed, your right foot will trail easily around and you will be able to do as many

Illustration 35

Illustration 36

revolutions as you wish. With practice you will be able to turn threes while pivoting, using all your edges, IF, OF, and IB, with variations on each. But right now the simple back pivot and the stop will do.

DANCE STEPS

Dance steps, for solo, pairs, fours, and larger groups constitute one of skating's never ending fascinations. New steps, new rhythms for old steps—no one skater will ever exhaust all the possibilities. It has been proved that audiences enjoy dance steps set to music as much as the skaters themselves; soloists and pairs who specialize only in well-timed steps with unexpected twists and turns and rhythm emphasis have won as much applause as the more spectacular performers. It is manifestly impossible for any book not entirely devoted to the subject to teach you many series of steps already woven into whole dances; but it is possible to give you a few of the individual moves and to suggest others. Besides, it's really much more fun for you to discover combinations for yourself, and —who knows?—perhaps you will run into one that no one has ever thought of before.

The waltz eight, the man's ten-step, the rolls, and the changes of edge, plus the threes you already know, form a broad foundation for building a repertoire of dance moves. As you become an advanced skater, you will insert the more difficult turns, brackets, counters, and rockers, and even loops, in bewildering array, but these combinations can hardly be called "primer" studies. For now you must confine yourself to the edges and turns you are studying—though "confine" is hardly the correct word, for you will be amazed to see how much you can do with them.

The Chassé and the Progressive

First, some very simple ways of stepping, each variation receiving its name from the placement of the feet during the steps—namely, the "chassé," the "progressive," the "cross roll." These are in addition to the cross behind and the crossover you already know. In the chassé, which like all the others may be done either backward or forward, the free foot takes the ice directly beside the skating foot, which then without any push rises from the ice a few inches either directly beside the new skating foot or slightly in front of it, before it in turn retakes the ice from a regulation push.

A progressive is so called because the free foot takes the ice beside the skating foot but during the actual stroke progresses beyond it, leaving the new free foot in a trailing position. The difference between this and a regular stroke is not only that the new foot advances but there is very little, if any, push involved. It is essentially a gliding move and should be done with a well-bent skating knee and a carefully extended free leg. This is a stroke that, forward or backward, looks easy but is deceptively difficult to perfect. (I've found a good rule of thumb is to slide the free heel down beside the skating toe on a forward progressive, and the free toe beside the skating heel on a backward one.) Be careful not to catch the picks of your skate as it comes off the ice behind a forward progressive.

Cross Rolls

Cross rolls are easier to do backward; they may be done forward, of course, but somehow don't seem as useful for solo work as for pairs. From a regular OB stroke, swing your free leg wide from front to back and cross it well over behind your skating foot onto another OB edge; repeat the free leg swing and the cross to OB several more times; add a quick push-away from a bent knee and ankle each time, plus a strong matching swing-back of the free arm and shoulder. Let your body sway with the curve from side to side, and there you have the famous "Dutch roll"—a skating figure hundreds of years old, originated, so they say, on the Zuider Zee and perpetuated in every country that skates.

Simple "shuffle" steps are good only when used in syncopated rhythm with the music. They are done like a repeated chassé, with the weight shifting from one short stroke to another, while the foot that is leaving the ice slips way forward, no matter in which direction you are skating. If the steps are done with flexible knees and swinging arms, you can get a quick jazz rhythm with them that is interesting if not over-done. In the same quick-rhythm style, you can gain speed and a good effect backward by a continuous repetition of 6, 7, 8, 9, 6, 7, 8, 9, etc., of the man's ten-step. Or you can change the timing of the steps to suit the tempo of the music, by holding certain steps and doubling up on others.

"Continuous change of edge" is just what its name implies, a series of one-foot changes of edge—inner to outer, outer to inner, etc.—skated right down the ice, or diagonally. It is noth-ing more nor less than a wiggly line made by quick knee action combined with body lean and free leg pull from side to side; but if you time it to the music, it is an amusing way to work into a pivot, a spin, or some other finishing figure. If you go backward, keep your free foot in back all the time as you change; if you go forward, keep your free foot in front. Either way point it out and down and "work" it in synchronization with your lean and your skating knee.

More Mohawks and Choctaws

There is another mohawk, from OF to OB, and there are two different types of "choctaws," which should be learned starting both right and left with varying positions of the free leg during and after the turns. (A choctaw is a method of turning around from one edge forward to the opposite edge backward, thus causing you to change circles, instead of turning around the same center as in the mohawks.)

The outside mohawk is admittedly difficult to do well; the outside choctaw is easy and has a fun swing to it. Let's tackle the mohawk first. Skate a LOF edge in regular first position, bend both knees, and bring the heel of the free skate to the inside of the heel and almost to the instep of the skating foot; just before changing feet and bringing the weight onto the ROB edge, reverse the shoulders even more strongly than for the inside mohawk; slide the left foot off the ice and press it hard back as the transition is made. To hold this ROB with any degree of ease, you must concentrate on a real lean to the right in the split second you turn, with your skating hip hard in, your back muscles taut, your skating knee flexible, and your weight on the skating shoulder and the ball of the foot. Contrary to school figure technique I even press my left *hip* back to match the pressure of the left shoulder; as long as I keep my hips tight, I find this parallel position easier to control here. Practice the OF mohawk starting right, even though it may be a form of self-punishment at first. Facility with it in both directions can lend variety to dance invention later on.

This outside mohawk may also be done with the free leg forward after the turn, as may the inside mohawk and both choctaws (in which case they are called "closed" turns). Instead of placing the free heel at the instep of the skate, you must now cut the turned-out right foot down close *behind* the heel of your left skate, so that as you shift weight, you may press the left leg instantly forward. Bend your knee well and feel as if you were about to turn a ROB three. (If you keep your hips square, you won't turn unless you want to!) All other directions for this mohawk are the same as for the preceding "open" outside mohawk where the free leg was held backward in the finishing position. It is thus entirely the free leg that differentiates between "open" and "closed" turns, i.e., finishing backward equals "open," forward equals "closed."

For a left outside choctaw skate a few strokes and then the 1, 2, 3 of the man's ten-step; hold 3 on a strong LOF, with your free arm leading and shoulders square; swing your right leg forward, at the same time letting your skating knee rise and your skating shoulder move forward; as the free leg reaches the apex of the swing, quickly reverse your shoulders and slide your turned-out free foot down close behind your left heel onto a strong inside backward edge; bend your right knee and ride away on the new circle with your left leg stretched in front, and your head looking back over your left shoulder. All the arm and shoulder movements for these mohawks and choctaws must be very decisive. For instance, here the right arm moves from a stretched backward position before the turn to a curved position across the front of the body after the turn; the left arm, of course, does the same in reverse order. Not only is this turn fun for the skater; it has a definite audience appeal if done with wide sweeping edges, a free use of the free leg combined with a lilt of the skating knee, and a definite body sway from one steady edge to the other.

Practice this choctaw now in both open and closed positions, with a swing of the free leg and without a swing of the free leg. The other—and more difficult—set of the choctaws involves turning from IF to OB edges, open and closed, with a swing and without a swing. On this turn, the shoulder reversal beforehand is so important in effecting the change of lean that if you forget to time it correctly, control of the edge afterward becomes almost impossible. On all choctaws there is a deep bend to start, a smoothly rising knee to the turn, and a deep bend away from it. Always practice all turns on both feet.

With these turns added to our dance equipment, we can go ahead now and work out sequences ad infinitum. I shall suggest a few; the rest is up to you, your observant eye when watching others skate, and your native ingenuity.

Salchow March

There is a nice little combination called the Salchow March (named for the first champion of the world in the modern style of skating). Step LFO, cross RIF in behind, then turn your left foot as for a mohawk and give a little hop onto LIB, step RBO, cross a short LOB behind, and then cross RIB over in front. Turn LOF, and repeat the whole sequence. A simple mazurka jump may be inserted after the fourth step, landing LOF and going into a repetition from there; or an even simpler IB toe jump, landing LOF, may be added after the complete series of steps before the repetition.

Long Dance

A sequence that I almost always teach beginning free skaters at the second test level is the "long dance," so called because, properly done, it covers the entire length and width of an ordinary rink. Start with the usual 1, 2, 3 of the man's ten-step on deep edges; on 3 sway your body with a change of edge to LIF, leaving your free leg in front during the change. (Henceforth I shall call this little change the "sway"—I like to use it frequently for rhythm and a slight pattern variation before mohawks, etc.) Now do RIF mohawk to LIB, and ROB (4, 5, 6), letting yourself rotate to the outside of the curve and your free leg go back on 6; step LIF, mohawk to RIB, and stroke LOB (4, 5, 6 in reverse), repeating the outward rotation on 6; make a short RIF, and then on a large arc do a LIF three followed at once by a ROF three; step wide (this is the first wide step I've taught you, except for a cross-over) to LIB and hold your free leg in front for two to three beats, and then finish off with 6, 7, 8, 9, 10 of the man's ten-step, swinging the leg forward with a nice knee rise on 10. From here you can ad-lib a finish, perhaps a big LOF swing choctaw, ending with a spiral or a jump.

As this dance has a mohawk sequence both ways, necessitating real edge lean and shoulder control, plus threes in controlled rotation, it is excellent training. It is also excellent fun, as the rhythm may be varied in any way that suits your fancy. It is equally adaptable to waltz, march, or fox trot time. It is good for pairs, fours, or larger groups for shadow skating down the side and across the ends of a rink; in fact, it was invented in Canada and taught to me by my husband, Guy Owen, as part of the famous Minto Four repertoire.

Mohawks in series will make effective continuous turning dance moves. Do 1, 2, 3, 4, 5, 6, of the man's ten-step; then turn onto LOF, repeat 4, 5, 6; repeat the LOF and the mohawk as many times as you want. The pattern will, of course, be circular. To straighten out the turns so that they may be done the length of the ice surface or on the diagonal, turn each time from ROB of the sixth step to a short LIF before repeating the mohawk. Dance steps like this depend on quick movement and lightness of knee-ankle action for their effect.

Instead of inside mohawks, you may use outside ones for a similar type of dance. LOF, RIF, LOF, RIF, LOF mohawk to

ROB, cross LIB in front, step RIF, LOF, repeat mohawk and crossover; then repeat this four-step turning sequence as many times as you wish.

Round Dance

For a good-looking round dance do the first six steps of the man's ten-step (including the sway on 3); then on 6 turn a ROB three to RIF followed by an inside mohawk to LIB, followed by another push to ROB and a three, followed by another mohawk from RIF to LIB, etc. Remember to do each move just as you have been taught to do it separately—in other words, rotate and check, rotate and check, leaning always to the center of the circle and using your free leg with great precision. If you combine this back three dance with the LOF mohawk circular dance just described, you can produce steps that turn first to the inside of the circle and then to the outside. Such variation is desirable, so that an onlooker can't always predict your rotation and hence become bored.

Cut-over threes done on the diagonal are good (of course, they don't *have* to be done on the diagonal, but you should train yourself to use all possible lines, angles, and curves of the ice surface). To do a cut-over three, turn a regular OF three; then on the IB roll over in a short change edge to OB, at the same time swinging your free leg around from back to front and placing it down on the IB crossed over in front of the skating foot. Press your free shoulder well back. Now turn onto the OF again and repeat. To do this figure on the diagonal, keep all your curves shallow, so that you can move easily from one edge to the next and still keep the general pattern a straight line. If you "snap" your three turns with a decisive movement of your shoulders and then let your whole body sway on the back edges, you will get rhythm and feeling into a move that might easily become stilted and static.

Chain Threes

Chain threes make another good figure. These, too, can be done either on a curve or a straight line. Turn an OF three, then an IB three, an OF three and an IB, etc. This is a continuous series of threes all on one foot, which is very good when well timed to the music. Be sure to swing the free foot vigorously and close past each turn to give the dance character. Be equally sure to press your free hip and shoulder hard back after each turn to give you control over it. "Snap" your turns quickly.

Spread eagles woven into plain steps always produce a pleasant variation, especially suited to men. Invent your own combinations, using the inner spread (Illus. 37) as well as the outer. Entry and exit steps may vary greatly, so let your imagination go.

One of the chief beauties of ice dancing is neat footwork and precise stepping. Each step should be distinct and articulate with the free foot *always* well stretched and well pointed. Each time you put your free foot on the ice, put it *close* to your skating foot ("touching" and "brushing" are safe rules for pushing and passing—remember?), for "straddling" is not only ugly in itself but will, as you must know by now, affect your whole position, ruining a simple dance as well as a complicated one. A skater who dances around on two feet is either a poor skater or a lazy one, and all the effectiveness of the moves is lost in a sloppy shuffle.

When you dance on ice, you must let your arms and hands flow with the movement of your body, observing the rules for curving and straightening that I gave you earlier. Let them be always flexible, and remember that your hands should look like an unobtrusive continuation of your arms. This means that they must not dangle, flop, wave up and down, pull up from the wrist, be stiff, or have any other kind of exaggerated position; it also means that you should hold your arms and hands gracefully away from your body so that they will constantly change position to fit with your steps and follow out the line of your back and your whole body. The body likewise must lean and flow with the edges. Your head should be as erect as your body, but it should turn naturally as the different directions and edges of the dance demand. There is nothing worse than seeing

Illustration 37

a skater do accomplished steps with his feet and yet keep his upper body and his arms so rigid that the whole effect is stiff and unpleasant. No matter how much such a skater may stroke on the *beat* of the music, he could never be said to be truly rhythmic.

A controlled bend, rise, bend of the skating knee and a flexible ankle, combined with clean steps and graceful body movements, will give your dancing a lilting quality, whether you have music to skate to or not. But if there *is* music and you don't listen to it and don't step to its rhythm, all will be in vain. A skater who can do all the steps but doesn't keep time is like a pianist who can play all the scales but no melody. Luckily most people can train themselves to keep time, even if they do not have a natural feeling for it; most stepping off beat is due to carelessness, or to such preoccupation with the steps that the skater fails to listen to the music at all! Unless you are one of those lucky naturals who find it impossible to get out of time—and there are not many of them—train yourself to move with the music no matter what you may be doing, plain skating or even school figures, for it will make all the difference not only to your own pleasure but to the pleasure your skating affords others.

BASIC SPINS

Spins are fun if you don't get dizzy and no fun at all if you do. Dizziness, however, can be overcome in almost all cases; in reality few people get really dizzy once they learn a handful of spinners' tricks. Most novices look down or look up when they start to spin; either one guarantees giddiness. Look straight out at eye level as you go round and let your eyes focus as normally as they can. Most novices also unwittingly rock their bodies forward or backward, or sideways, or all three when they first spin, and this is like deep-sea fishing in a ground swell—you feel a funny motion and you don't like it. Once you learn how to center a spin, you must concentrate on keeping your shoulders level and both your body and your head perfectly still as you revolve. A most effective finishing trick is to stop your spin with a jerk, jabbing one toe point in the ice and giving your head a definite toss to clear away the cobwebs.

The plainest, most unvarnished spin and the best one to teach you how to revolve is the "double flat-foot." This is a two-foot spin which traces big ringlets on the ice. On the assumption that you are right-handed and that you feel most comfortable revolving to the left, I shall describe the spin in this direction. But as soon as you know how to center, you must do some experimenting on your own to find out whether this is your natural direction of rotation. Almost everyone turns more easily one way than the other, and when you come to turning in the air in any jump that requires more than a half-revolution, the question becomes vitally important. Learn to spin and jump in the same direction from the beginning and your whole free skating life will be easier. I have had pupils come to me who had learned spins in one direction and simple jumps in the other, who could never learn to master double-revolution jumps or the complicated jump spins. Of course there are a lucky few who are ambilateral and find it equally easy to jump and spin in both directions. If you are among this number, cultivate your good fortune right from the start.

To enter the double flat-foot, turn a ROF three, put down a short LOB, and crossover wide to a deep RIB, allowing your free arm to go way forward and your free foot back across the print. Now bring your turned out left heel way inside the circle and step onto a very deep LOF edge with a well-bent knee and a strong body lean to the center. Keep your balance on the center of your blade and hard over a pressed-in skating hip. Start to draw your left arm back as you step in, and lean until you feel you must make a three. At this point (your edge should at least have come around to face the point where you stroked into it), quickly straighten your body up and allow your free leg to swing out wide to the side. As your left skate catches the IB edge after a small turn, bring your right skate down beside the left, about 6 inches away, toed in, and also on a very slight inside edge. This whole straightening move is a matter of split seconds. Properly placed, your feet feel as if they were chasing each other around a little tub, the right foot on the IF chasing the left foot on the IB edge! Your body weight should be absolutely evenly divided between your two feet, and once you begin to spin, there must not be the slightest movement of your feet, nor any movement of the trunk of the body above them.

By winding up to the right on your preparation and then snapping up straight from a deep lean after starting a windup action to the left, plus the wide swinging of the free leg before it draws quickly down into place, you create so much spinning momentum that your body will turn a few times without further movement. As you feel your original momentum diminishing, your arms start their job of keeping you going.

On the "centering up," the arms stretch out, shoulder high, to each side. (It is well to clench your fists right then to prevent a subsequent rush of blood to the fingers, a common malady that feels like "pins and needles.") After a few turns curve the elbows and draw your fists together in front of you in a circular movement. This should be a gradual "fighting" move, with one set of muscles pulling and another set of muscles resisting the pull. Once met, your hands should draw in to your chest, your elbows bent out, and from there they slowly push straight and close down your body. As your arms push down, your shoulders should push down, too, and your head should push back up against them. Pull your abdominal muscles in and your diaphragm up. This is the *only* body movement that won't throw you off balance; when done right, it will give you a long, fast spin. This method of maintaining speed is common to all fast standing spins.

If you find the entry described above too difficult at first, you may start from a single push onto a deep RIF edge and snap up straight from there, allowing your left foot to toe in to place. Actually any description of how to snap into a spin is useless unless you practice sufficiently yourself to get the "feel" of it.

The "single flat-foot" spin is the basic one-foot spin and is beautiful when well done. There is something very satisfying about seeing a skater revolve smoothly on one foot in the same place, with a frictionless ease that works up greater and greater speed. I feel it important to learn flat spins before toe spins, as spinning on the flat of the blade is basic to so many other types of spin (cross-foot, sit spin, arabesque, etc.); a skater who learns to spin on the toe first often finds it difficult to center on the flat. On *all* spins do *not* scratch on the preparation edges.

The preparation is the same as the first method for the double flat-foot, except that, when you come to the point where you want to turn, you straighten up sharply and center your balance on the ball of your foot on the absolute *flat* of your skate. This time you do not allow your skate to turn at all, but center up while your body is still going *forward*. There should be no edge of any sort while you spin, neither slight outer nor slight inner. As you center from a strong OF edge, swing your well-turned out free leg forward wide and high, keeping it straight out from your hip to the right side as you begin the spin. Bend your free knee, with your foot straight down at right-angles from the knee. As you draw your arms in for speed, bend the free knee farther so that the free foot is placed directly *behind* your spinning knee. This is a resistance move and will give you tremendous speed. If your balance holds steady, you will be able to add still more speed and length by dropping this free foot slowly down the back of your spinning leg until both feet are closed in together. Keep pressure back on the spinning shoulder blade, but do not turn the upper body at all.

The last absolute essential for a good spin—and in many ways this is the most important of all—is a *straight spinning knee* (or knees if it's a two-foot spin). Learning to spin with a bent knee is the most common fault of beginners, and one of the most disastrous, for it is difficult to break. *All spins should revolve on one spot,* but if you learn to spin with a bent skating knee you will always "travel" and you will find it exceedingly difficult to keep from rocking back and forth. Here my continual admonition to bend the skating knee must be put into complete reverse: Straighten it as much as possible, even to springing it back in "locked" position. Have your friends tell you whether your knee is *really* straight, for there is nothing so hard to determine yourself (I get a spinning knee checkup regularly, for my knee, even today, is often slightly bent although I feel perfectly sure it is like a ramrod!)

Toe spins, both fast and slow, are highly effective. The preparation and principles for the fast "scratch spin" are the same as for the single flatfoot; instead of centering on the flat, you raise onto the *first* toe point of your skate (Illus. 38). You will scratch out little circles on the ice—hence the name. This time you do not bring your free foot *behind* your spinning knee to increase speed, *but in front of it,* gradually lowering your leg until your feet are crossed at the ankle. To do a slow scratch spin, keep your arms away from the body with the free arm forward and the skating arm back in spiral position, extend your turned out free leg as high as possible behind, keep your shoulders level, arch your back, and hold your head erect. If this position is maintained with an unwavering free leg and arms until you are turning very slowly, it can be a most effective spin for both men and women.

The "sit spin," or "Jackson Haynes"—as it should properly be called in honor of the father of modern skating who invented it—is a more athletic form of spinning, which increases in difficulty in direct ratio to the age of the skater who is trying to learn it (although I have found many children too stiff to do it at all and many adults who could do it right away). The correct position of the spin is a squat, with the free leg extended straight out in front and the rest of the body doubled over a completely bent skating leg. (The model in Illus. 39 is spinning on her right foot, so all directions must be transposed.) The revolutions are made on the flat of the skate, which means that, to maintain balance, the spinning ankle must be bent way forward, the knee bent to the maximum, and the hip jackknifed. The upper part of the spinning leg should actually rest against the calf of the same leg. To hold this position, the weight of the body has to be balanced forward to the absolute limit.

The preparation is essentially the same as for the single flatfoot. On the LOF entry edge you must lean way forward (39-1), straightening your knee *very slightly* as you start to center

Illustration 39

Illustration 38

(39-2), and then bending at once *quickly* into the deep-knee squat position, as you simultaneously whip your free leg from back to front wide around to the side (39-3). This free leg *must* end its swing *directly in front* of your spinning foot (39-4); if it stops at all to the side, you will topple over. Point your free toe down, turning it well out, too, so that the outside of your free foot is toward the ice; hold your free skate with both hands or with your skating hand while the free hand either rests on the free knee or is held out for balance; make sure that your backbone is straight, not hooped over; keep your head in line with your back (39-4); do all that and you will have a good Jackson Haynes position. If you hit dead center on the flat of your blade at the ball of your foot, you can spin fast and almost interminably like this.

To be a versatile spinner, you must also learn to spin in the same rotation on the other foot. These are called "back spins," although the preparation is from a deep IF edge and there is *no* turn to the back edge at all. The basic back flat spin is done in the exact position of the IF edge. Wind up first by doing a strong LIF, rotating the shoulders hard as you bring the free foot forward, and then step into a deep RIF with your skating hip way in under you. Keep your free arm in front and your whole body square as your edge curves sharply in. At the point of centering, straighten up quickly. Your free knee remains bent almost beside your straight spinning knee, and your free hip muscles contract hard to keep the pressure on this side forward against the rotation. Turn out your free leg from the knee down. Now consciously pull back on your free thigh muscles against the muscles that are holding the hip forward. This internal resistance pressure of the free leg added to your original momentum will produce good speed even without pulling in the arms.

Back toe spins (with the free leg closing in in front) and back sit spins should be learned by all those expecting to go on to advanced free skating. A "camel spin" (which should be called an arabesque spin, since there should be *no* hump in the back!) may be tried by all those with a good arched arabesque position.

Preparation is the same as for the standing flat foot, except that the edges are even deeper. Centering is on the toe point with a bent knee for *one turn,* before dropping the skate to the flat and stiffening the spinning knee. *The body must be well forward on the entry edge and stay there as you center the spin.* Draw the skating arm and shoulder back as you hit the center and contract all the muscles of your back, at the same time pressing your free leg back as hard as possible. This spin takes a good deal of practice to perfect and should not be tried at all if your spiral position is poor, as all errors of form become compounded in the spin.

BASIC JUMPS

Many youngsters seem to think that jumps are practically the whole of figure skating, which you by this time realize is hardly the case. On the other hand, jumping, whether from a springboard, a ski run, or a pair of skates, is about the nearest to flying the human body ever comes, and it is a wonderfully exhilarating feeling.

To get this feeling of flying, you must take off from a speedy edge and get plenty of elevation. Long, low jumps, "skimmers" as they are called, may be technically all right, but they are not so thrilling either to watch or to do. A second of poised suspension in the air, where for a breathless instant the skater seems to be held up by an outside force—that is the jumper's ideal. The late Guy Owen, one of the world's great jumpers, used to lift so high and poise so long on one of the simple back toe jumps I am going to teach you that audiences used to gasp and wonder when he was going to come down!

To comparatively few, however, is this ability to "hang in the air" given. I am convinced many more skaters could acquire it if they would learn to elevate high from the ground and then apply the same principles to the ice. Whatever the surface of take-off, the knees must bend deeply for a *quick upward* spring, while the whole body and the head remain erect and centered, back straight and diaphragm drawn up. Breathing in at the moment of take-off is also a help toward "levitation." Men are naturally better jumpers than women, because the spring itself takes strength as well as timing. As a whole, however, each new generation of girl skaters jumps better than the last, and the progress from the dainty little long-skirted hops of only a few generations ago to the daring double-revolution jumps of to-day is amazing.

As with everything you have tackled so far, the simple jumps come before the complicated ones; the same principles apply to both, and once you have mastered one set, you are well on the way toward mastering the other.

Simplest of all is the "bunny hop." This is merely a forward leap from the flat of one skate to the toe pick of the other, and back to the flat of the original take-off skate. When well done, however, with speed and height, it can be most effective, while it is so easy that any skater of literally any age can do it. After a few short strokes, take a straight LF with the skating knee well bent and the free leg extended behind (count 1); now (count 2) spring quickly, flexing the ankle so that you lift straight up from the picks of your left skate, at the same time swinging your free leg straight forward and up past your left leg (the spring plus the swing will give you an upward thrust plus forward momentum); as your left leg leaves the ice, kick it *slightly* backward, so that at the top of the leap your legs will be in a semisplit position; now let your weight shift onto your right toe point as you descend, some little distance ahead of where you took off; bend that knee and, as your left leg comes forward past this toe point, *push* onto the flat of your left skate again and ride away. The toe-point and edge landing should *not* be simultaneous (a common fault in forward toe-point landings) but should be counted like a half note and a whole note (or short, long = u—). Now practice the same hop from the right flat to the left toe point. Your arms should swing with the jump (left arm forward with the left-footed spring, and vice versa) but should not rise above the shoulder line, while the shoulders themselves must not rise at all—on this, or any other jump, ever, amen.

The fundamental edge jump is the "waltz jump" (Illus. 40),

sometimes also called a "three jump," though this is a misnomer as there is a real "jumped three" which you will learn shortly. In a waltz jump you take off from the OF edge, turn a half-turn in the air, and land on the OB of the other foot. You see, it is like the first two edges of the waltz eight, with the jump substituting for the three turn on the ice (a majority of the basic jumps correspond to a figure on the ice).

The first six steps of the man's ten-step make a good preparation for the take-off. (If you are one of those, usually left-handed, who revolve easier from right to left, start the steps on the right foot, progressing to the right, and reverse all the directions.) Hold 6 on a deep knee bend, change into the ROB spiral position with a strong upward draw of the skating knee, and then bend again as the skating foot changes to a slight IB edge and the free foot comes down close for the push to LOF. Push vigorously to a well-bent left leg which holds for one count before the skating knee snaps straight (40-1) and the whole body "lifts" from a flexed ankle. The right leg meanwhile, from a straight backward position at the start of the LOF (caution: it is most important that this free leg not fall back inside the curve after the ROB to LOF push), swings forward in a wide arc, toe turned slightly in and knee straight (40-1). All the preparatory edges so far should have been skated on the same wide-angle curve, and now you should aim to land *outside* this curve (40-2). This will prevent too much rotation and subsequent loss of balance when you land. The whole movement, from the turn to LOF to the spring, should be *quick* (count 1, 2). You should feel that you are wound up like a coil (that's your knee bend), and then suddenly let go. As soon as you leave the left toe on the take-off, move your left leg at once up and back along the same arc your right leg transcribed (40-2, 3, 4). At the apex of the jump your body is facing straight in toward the center of the ice with both your feet wide apart but at an even height underneath you (40-3). Both legs, needless to say, should be straight and toes pointed to avoid an unpleasant "frog" look in mid-air.

At the top of the jump allow your body weight to shift

Illustration 40

toward your right side (40-4) so that as you complete the half-revolution, you can land softly over the ball of your right foot with your skating hip already tucked tight in underneath you (40-5, 6). If you continue the backward movement of the left leg smoothly, it will be slightly back of and to the outside of the right leg at the moment of the ROB landing (40-6). Be sure that you tighten the muscles of the whole free leg and buttocks so that the hips will remain firmly square and this free leg will not fall in behind you after landing. In fact, on this entire landing edge you should feel as if your free foot were pointing to the outside of the ice surface (40-7) (to the barrier of the rink —or the edge of the pond—as you lean strongly inward). That is one of the best control tips I know. For if your free leg curls around behind you toward the inside of the curve, you will find that this rotation plus your momentum will make it impossible for you to hold your landing edge at all. At best you will have to hop off it; at worst you will fall down.

Remember: No jump is any better than the control of its landing edge. A jump is judged first by this, second by elevation and position in the air, once a correct take-off has been made.

How do you make yourself revolve in the air? Simple. The problem with most jumping is how *not* to revolve too far! Two main factors influence this revolution: the use of your arms and shoulders and the use of your jumping leg after the take-off. For a half-turn or even a whole turn, nothing more than a simple reversal of the arms and shoulders is needed—no flailing or exaggerated pulling in is necessary. In fact, on edge jumps if the jumping leg works backward after the spring, this alone is often enough to turn the body.

Thus, if turning the shoulders provides the mechanics of turning the body, then it stands to reason that the shoulders must *not* turn until the body *is leaving* the ice. In all jump take-off positions the shoulders must be held against the revolution of the jump until the split second of spring. *Ergo,* in this waltz jump of ours your left arm and shoulder should lead and the free arm and shoulder should be pressed back until the actual thrust from the ice. As the right leg swings forward, the right arm swings forward above it and the left arm simultaneously starts a backward movement. The landing finds the skating arm forward, the free arm back, and the head looking back over the free shoulder in orthodox OB spiral position.

The landing of all jumps should be soft and flexible, with the edge on a wide-angle curve that matches the curve that preceded the take-off. Softness is achieved, first, through exact balance at the moment of impact and, second, through the use of the skating knee. Your knee is your shock-absorber; keep it stiff and you will jar your whole body; make it flexible (40-6, 7) with a bending and rising motion and you will ride away lightly and airily. My husband used to say that jumps should land on a *bending* knee; that is, as the skate touches the ice, the knee is partially bent and continues to bend more as the edge continues; when it is fully bent, it at once begins to straighten slowly and gradually. This continual working of the skating knee gives a quality of "flight" to skating. Landing on a completely bent knee that stays bent can be just as jarring as landing on a stiff one.

Letting out the skating hip is the most common reason for a "broken" landing. Leaning out of the circle will have the same effect. However, by the same token, the upper body must not break into the curve either. The body must remain one unit throughout. Before the take-off the body weight must remain back, shifting forward up over the take-off foot only on the thrust. There must be absolutely no forward break of the body at the hips or waist on the take-off edge. Returning to the technique of the waltz jump, you will see that it is started from an orthodox outside eight first position and landed on an orthodox outside backward eight second position, with all the controls of those edges exercised to the full because of the momentum of the jump itself. (Note: the model here has landed with his shoulders square, but in the next few feet moved his skating shoulder forward, free shoulder back, and head over his free shoulder).

I have dwelt at such length on the waltz jump because it teaches so exactly the basic theory of all jumping. The general instructions apply no matter what the edge of take-off, inside or outside, forward or backward—namely, a wide-angle preparation, a straight upward thrust from a well bent-knee, no rotation of the shoulders before the take-off, aiming the jump toward the outside of the circle, a straight body at all times, movement of the head with the rotation of the jump, weight over the landing leg with the skating hip in and the skating knee *bending* and rising for a controlled ride-out. For extra spring my husband always said that he felt as if he "snapped" his back as well as his knee at the take-off of every jump.

Many instructors teach a strong "checking" of the rotation of a jump through the shoulders—even to thrusting the free shoulder forward on landing—but I feel that the major check must always be through the back and hips. If the free hip is pressed hard forward with a strong muscular contraction, this will give sufficient control for all but double- and triple-revolution jumps, provided all the other requirements of a straight back and balanced edges are observed. On double-revolution jumps, where the rotation requires a definite pulling in of the arms, a square shoulder position with the arms out to the side, as the landing foot touches the ice, often gives added control.

Most unattractive of all the jumping errors is the prevalent habit of looking down at the ice before, during, and after jumping. Not only does it destroy a sense of true balance but it makes the skater look unsure of himself, whether he feels so or not. I always think that a skater who constantly looks back at the spot where he landed is mentally saying, "Did I really get around? Did I really land all right?" Such an attitude appeals to neither audiences nor judges!

Skating jumps are of essentially two categories, those that take off one foot from a running edge and those that add the toe point of the free foot as a lever at the take-off. The latter are commonly called "toe jumps" and the most basic of these is the "mohawk," or "half-flip," jump.

After a few quick strokes (plus a bunny hop perhaps) take a straight right forward edge and hop a quick mohawk turn onto a straight left back edge (this may also be done on a curve with a definite RIF edge to LIB). Immediately on turning the mohawk, bend the left knee, hold the left shoulder and arm firmly forward and the right shoulder and arm straight back, with your head forward and your eyes looking along your left arm. At the same instant extend your right leg back from the turn, rigidly straight-kneed and with the front of the knee facing the ice. Do not raise it more than a few inches. The hips should be tucked forward under you and the back kept perfectly straight, with the muscles at the base of the spine pulled down as this right leg reaches back.

Now in an absolutely simultaneous action, place your toe point in the ice and snap the left knee for the take-off. As the left leg pushes up, the right leg gives a simultaneous *forward pull,* so that the left foot rides back to the right and the body weight shifts back up over the toe points as the body rises into the air. The stiff right leg thus acts much as a pole does to a pole vaulter. If the timing is exact, the feet will be close together all during the jump. Turn the body and the head a half-revolution to the left, landing forward just as for the right-footed bunny hop—that is, on the left toe point, pushing off onto a well-controlled RIF edge in regulation spiral position (first position of the IF eight). There is so little effort in making this half-turn that it is not necessary to move the arms and shoulders at all—the left can remain forward and the right back through-out—but if you wish to add another half turn, you must draw your left shoulder back and your right forward at the moment of take-off. If you *do* add the half-turn, you will be doing a full "flip jump," which lands on the ROB edge in the exact way that the waltz jump landed. However, I must again counsel you to make haste slowly. Perfect the technique of your plain mo-hawk jump before adding any variations. It is this technique that will produce not only the flip jump, the flip-and-a-half, and the double flip but the split jump and the split flip. If the basic jump is not right, none of these advanced variations will be right either. In fact, some of them you may never be able to do at all. Of course, I am talking to the young and daring now; those not so athletic, however, can certainly do the mohawk jump well both to left and right—and, if limber, will be able to add the split jump, too. All these same jumps may be pre-pared from a straight line three turn in place of a mohawk.

Quick timing is again an essential ingredient of a successful toe jump. Try counting the whole preparation: 1 for the edge before the mohawk, 2 for the turn and the edge out (the bend and reach), and 3 for the actual spring. Even though the action of the toe-point leg is vitally important, the main "lift" still comes from the straightening snap of the well-bent skating knee. Be sure that this skate remains on a good running edge and that there is not the slightest scraping on the toe point be-fore the jump. "Stopping up" on the points not only is technically very bad but it takes away all the appearance of freedom and joy. Scraping like this makes an unpleasant noise, and I often say to beginning toe jumpers, "If you can *hear* the edge before you jump, don't jump," for the habit of scratching, once acquired, seems very difficult to break. As for the landing, you should be able to hold it a full circle without turning. If you observe all the rules of position and do not allow the body to pitch forward on the landing (another common error), you should have no problems of control.

The "ballet jump" (see Illus. 34-A at start of Chapter VII) looks advanced and makes a lovely picture, but is really an elementary jump that can be done well by anybody at any age. It takes little daring and depends mainly on good form for its effect. Again our favorite six steps (add a sway after 3 this time, just for fun), and when you stroke onto the ROB of 6, let your free leg go quickly back and turn your whole body to the left in the finishing OB spiral position (skating knee moderately straight at this point). Now bend deeply and reach your turned out and pointed left leg, hard back and very *slightly* outside the curve (see Illus. 41-1). Place the left toe point in the ice, at the same time bending that left knee (41-2); allow some of your body weight to shift to the left leg and spring from both legs. As your body (which turns forward as you place your toe in the ice) shoots straight up into the air, lift your right leg, turned out and pointed, high in the back and stretch your left leg straight down and slightly forward. Land on the left toe point and push off to a standard RIF spiral. Try the same jump from the LOB in the opposite direction. It is not difficult to reverse this one (Illus. 34-A).

The arms may strike a variety of poses in the air. I like to put my right arm forward and the left backward during the elevation, reversing them immediately upon landing. But you may throw both backward, or one upward over your head, etc. Whatever you do, it is wise to study the position before a mirror off the ice to see its effect for yourself. If instead of extending your left leg straight when you are in the air, you bend it so that your left knee is well forward while your right leg

rises straight back as in the ballet jump, you will be doing the so-called "stag," or "fawn," jump (Illus. 34-B). Again, on all these various toe jumps, be extra careful not to "scratch" your take-off edge. The model is a reverse (or left-to-right) jumper.

This same OB toe point take-off (where the extended free toe jabs the ice *outside* the line of the circle (Illus. 41-1, 2) —rather than inside it, as in the mohawk jump) has many variations. The plain ROB back toe jump (which my husband performed so fantastically) takes off just like the ballet jump, but this time both feet draw together in the air as the body stays facing out. Land on the right toe point and push off on your LOF. If you should throw your right leg forward at the take-off and the left leg back, so that they are crossed in the air, you will be doing the "mazurka jump" (41-3, 4, 5) (which you may insert into the Salchow march step—remember?). The mazurka is another photographer's delight, for it makes a fine picture in midflight. Done fast and with snapped-back elevation, as Tenley Albright did it, there is a thrill to it. But don't be afraid to try it, beginners; it's not as hard as it looks. Just think of doing a bunny hop as you swing your right foot forward past your left. Land right (toe) and push left (edge)—that's all there is to it (41-6, 7).

Two more important edge jumps come in the elementary

5

6

7

Illustration 41

category. They are the Salchow and the loop jump. As the Salchow (Illus. 42) is distinctly the easier to learn (though perhaps the more difficult to perfect), we will tackle that first. It is
an advance over the waltz jump in that it has a take-off from
the inside back edge and calls for a three-quarter revolution
of the body in the air. Prepare by skating fast and then doing a
big ROF roll. Step onto a very shallow LOF edge straight down
the ice and snap a quick left three, passing the free leg close
by the turn and pressing the free shoulder and the free hip hard
back after it (42-1). Hold this shallow LB edge (caution: don't
raise your free leg here) for one count thus, and then sink
quickly onto a deeply bent LIB edge (42-2, 3) which curves in
as you let your right leg (well turned out, straight, and pointed)
swing around in a wide arc. As your right foot comes forward
low to the ice and opposite your skating foot (42-3) (but several
feet to the inside of it), spring from your left knee (42-4). At this
point your right leg lifts up past your left, knee bending
slightly; your right arm and shoulder follow the action of the
right leg exactly (42-1, 2, 3, 4); and your body lifting after it
completes a loop in the air (42-5, 6, 7) and lands on the ROB
edge in finishing position (42-8) (left arm back, right arm forward, left leg back, and head looking around over the left

8   7   6   5

Illustration 42

shoulder). The general pattern of the jump is straight (not circular, as is so often taught), and after the curve of the take-off edge, the aim of the jump is again outside the circle in a continuation of the preceding edges (42-1, 8). Be careful to keep your skating hip hard in with your body weight over it and on your skating shoulder all the time you are preparing your take-off (42-1, 2, 3, 4). Leaning into your circle on the IB will take your weight off your skate, so that you will do a "spinner" rather than an elevated lift from a clean back edge. Also be careful that your body does not dip forward with a resultant scratch on the toe before the take-off. Any of these errors will destroy the possibility of eventually doubling the revolutions.

Knee action and rhythm are the keynotes of a successful Salchow. Count 1 as you *bend* on the LOF, count 2 as you snap the straight three and hold with a *straight* knee on the IB, count 3 as you *bend* on the curved LIB (42-2, 3), count 4 as you snap your take-off (42-4).

The outside backward "loop jump" (or "Rittberger," as it should be called for the fine skater and sportsman who invented it) finds the body transcribing a full loop in the air from an outside backward edge take-off on the right foot to an outside backward edge landing on the same foot. In other words, this is the first full-revolution jump you have learned. At first the take-off seems frightening, and for a while the

3   2   1

thought of a possible three-point landing on the back of the head is an ever present, though not very real, specter. I used to be allowed to take off and land on both feet for confidence in getting the "feel" just at first; and you may, too, if you promise not to do it very long.

After a few strokes—not too fast at first—turn a RIF mohawk, holding the LIB in firm checked position (left shoulder forward, right shoulder and hip hard back). Now bring the feet together, bending both knees, and push onto a deep-kneed ROB edge (exact position of the start of the OB eight); after one count, spring straight up backward from your right leg, snapping the knee completely straight. At the same instant (count 2) the left leg which has been strongly forward, turned out but with thighs touching, starts revolving backward in a moderately wide arc around the right leg. The left arm also starts moving backward and the right shoulder forward, so that by the time your right skate touches the ice again, you are completely around in the finishing position of the OB eight. Even your head, from looking back in over the right shoulder on the take-off, turns with the rotation so that on landing, it is looking back out over your left shoulder. Observe all rules for square hips, soft knees, straight back, etc., and you will have little trouble mastering this jump. Make sure you balance (without leaning) forward, jumping from and landing on the front of your skate (but not the teeth). Any backward pitch of the body or of the balance is to be avoided at all costs! If you do this jump correctly with speed and spring, you will achieve distance as well as height. However, it is easy to rotate the shoulders or hips—or both—before taking off, all of which will cause the edges, and hence the jump, to curl in. If you find this happening, check the position of your free arm and leg before the spring to make sure they are in front of you. And check the timing of your spring; if you delay, uncontrolled rotation is almost inevitable. No skater who has not perfected light, clean edges on both sides of the jump and achieved a feeling of real backward upward elevation should even think of doubling the turns in the air.

This same jump may be done to an IB landing on the left leg. Though it is then called a "half loop jump," this is a misnomer, as the body actually turns a complete revolution. There is less spin, however, as the left leg this time reaches out on the take-off and semisplits as it moves back and out of the circle. Extend the right leg back as the body turns in the air, so that on landing, it is already straight behind the left skate. Press the right shoulder and arm hard back over it, so that you ride away from the landing in the exact position of the finish of an OF three, completely parallel and checked along the circle. Keep your weight on your skating shoulder and lean in with a straight body line—and you won't find this a difficult jump. One of my partners did it with such velocity and stretch that he could cover 18 to 20 feet in a beautiful semisplit elevation!

If you do have trouble controlling the landing of the half-loop, practice the simple LOF three jump first. Take off a simple LOF edge, swinging your free leg forward and up close by your jumping leg. Turn this right leg strongly out in mid-air and press it back from the hip as your body does a half-revolution and lands on the LIB. Check your right arm and shoulder back as your left again moves in front. If you *skate* this relatively simple maneuver, you will be surprised to find what lift and "float" you can get from it.

For the young and limber, a "split jump" is an elementary move. But it never ceases to be spectacular at any level of skating if it is well done with true elevation and a hip-high split; like the little girl with the little curl, however, if it is bad, it is horrid, and is better left out of any program. The take-off position is identical to that of the plain mohawk jump. As the feet ride together at the take-off, kick the left leg forward and the right back straight from the hips. The forward leg should turn out and point, ditto the back leg. The left arm comes strongly past, as the whole body turns forward in the direction of flight on the take-off. The right arm flings back and stays there, even as you land, first on the left toe point and then the RIF edge. Leave your right leg up as long as possible and don't try to shift forward to land. Let your left skate land naturally without reaching for the ice. Success depends on a straight back on the take-off and a perfectly even balance between your two legs in the air. Leaning forward with your hips back, a "sway" back, or any other break in erect posture will ruin the timing and balance of this—or, for that matter, any other toe jump. Overreaching with the toe point leg so that there is a separation at the hips is fatal to quick strong elevation. Always feel as if a large rubber band were holding your hips together; stretching at the take-off is in the free knee and ankle only. Needless to say, your split jump will be as good as your split on the ground, and no better. So if you don't have a perfect floor split, limber, limber, and limber some more. Practice holding the landing edge without turning an IF three.

With the basic jumping knowledge you now have it will be quite possible for you to work out for yourself a proper method for executing many other jumps—for instance, an "Axel Paulsen jump" or a "Lutz jump." To do an Axel Paulsen you take off from an OF edge (as in a waltz jump), rotate one and a half turns in the air (similar left leg rotation movement to the loop jump), and land on the OB edge of the other foot (as in the waltz jump). Simultaneously with the spring, the right leg, with knee bent as if climbing a stair, kicks straight forward and up (not in an arc); the right arm comes forward to meet the left in front of you, both arms pull in as in a spin, and both check out for the landing (either square to the side or skating shoulder forward, free shoulder back, according to which method suits you best).

A Lutz jump takes off from an OB edge in a toe-point position identical to that for the flip jump. But as the rotation in the air is counter to the rotation of the take-off edge (in other words, if you are on a LOB, you turn to the left in the air), strong use must be made of the shoulders to complete the full turn before landing on the OB edge of the opposite foot. All the timing of the toe-point leg as lever is the same as for the flip.

Again I say: Practice all your positions and movements for jumps without your skates before you transfer them to the ice.

PROGRAM CONSTRUCTION

Without doubt, at this point you have sufficient ability to construct a program of continuous free skating that will give you a thrill to perform. More important, it will give a great deal of pleasure to those who watch you. Once a small degree of mastery is attained, skating should not be an introspective, self-centered exercise. It has inherent qualities of theater, and these you are now ready to explore.

First you must choose music. For your "maiden" program, choose something essentially simple, melodic, and with marked rhythm. Above all, choose something *you* like. A record of two to two and a half minutes is enough for now.

From the variety of spirals, spins, jumps, spread eagles (I hope!), and dance steps you have learned, choose only those you know you can do well. There is no pleasure for anyone in a display of half-mastered maneuvers. Listen to your music until you know every nuance before you begin to compose the program. There are certain established principles of good composition that you must know and use, but beyond them the sky's the limit. Use your ingenuity to the full.

Even the simplest program must have pattern. You must have a good opening and a good closing—in other words, a good first impression and a good last impression. That is rule number 1. So decide the two moves you do the very best; allocate one to the start and one to the finish. *How* you work them in will depend of course a good deal on the arrangement of the music.

The rest of your specialties should be spread throughout the routine, woven together into an artistic patterned whole by means of dance steps and well-posed edges. You should utilize the whole ice surface (unless you are on a large pond, of course), neglecting neither one end nor the other nor the middle. Diagonal moves and center figures that move across the ice lend variety and should not be neglected. It is boring to watch a skater moving always in one direction. You can gain interest, too, by varying the tempo of your moves; some may be slow to contrast with the speed of most of the program, but they must always be in keeping with the music. In a rink with a barrier make sure all your moves stay within easy sight of all the spectators. Don't dance too close to the sides or to the ends, or someone is sure to miss part of what you are doing.

The main thing is to present your program and yourself as well as you can. Remember you are yourself, an individual not quite like anyone else; so your performance must have the stamp of your individuality and personality, your own, not quite like anyone else's.

VIII

Four Ice Dances

As was intimated in the introduction, ice dancing is the reason many figure skaters take up the sport in the first place. To such an enthusiast all the practice of the basic edges and turns is just the means to the end of becoming a really good ice dancer. There is no doubt about it—good dancing is good fun.

Even those who know nothing about skating, who have never in their lives had on a pair of skates, know that an ice waltz is a thing of rare beauty. The fame of the waltz is universal and justly deserved. Fortunately or unfortunately, according to whether you are a purist or not, the waltz is wonderful fun for everyone who skates it. Even those waltzers who jerk their edges, pull their partners, are unsteady on their feet, and invariably step on the off beat of the music, go through the dance with a rapt expression of pleasure on their faces. Those skaters who are experts at the swaying moves and lilting rhythm give great enjoyment not only to themselves but to all who watch them.

Ice dancing, however, is by no means confined to the waltz. There are many other dances—many on elementary and intermediate levels—which should be learned before the famous waltz, which in skating terminology is known as the "American waltz." There are not only other and simpler waltzes but also dances to tango, march, and fox-trot time, which lead you gradually through the varying turns and positions to the greater intricacies of the advanced dances. Already there are great numbers of dances, and more are being composed and publicized all the time. All are available in diagram form in the official United States Figure Skating Association rule book and in the excellent little booklet "Ice Dances," both of which are published by the magazine *Skating* and may be obtained by writing to that publication at 30 Huntington Avenue, Boston, Massachusetts.

For the present purpose—to give you who are just beginning a working knowledge of the most important steps and rhythms —only four dances will be described: the elementary "Dutch waltz," the intermediate "fiesta tango," the lively "fourteen-step," and of course *the* waltz. The form of each has been standardized by the Dance Committee of the United States Figure Skating Association for use in tests and competitions, and though there are many variations possible in the timing and execution of each, these standardized versions are the easiest to assimilate.

Before studying the diagrams it would be well to do a quick review of the steps and turns (chassé, progressive, cross roll, mohawks, and choctaws) in Chapters III, IV and VII. These are all part of the dancer's equipment, although not all appear in the four dances under present scrutiny.

DUTCH WALTZ

This is a simple dance for beginners, consisting of forward steps only, with the partners skating side by side. Once you have mastered your outside forward rolls alone, find yourself a partner of equal or, preferably, greater proficiency. The steps are so deliberately simple that you will be able to concentrate on getting the feel of unifying your steps with another skater in rhythm to the music.

The hold for the partners finds the lady on the right of the man (of course two people of the same sex can dance this also!). With his right arm behind her back, he places his right hand on the lady's right hip. She puts her right thumb inside his palm and holds his hand firmly. She extends her left arm straight across the front of his body, and he holds her left hand in his left hand at a comfortable height. The man should give firm support and be in a position so close that his right hip will touch the lady's left hip.

After two short left, right strokes the dance starts in a corner and proceeds lengthwise down the ice before crossing over the

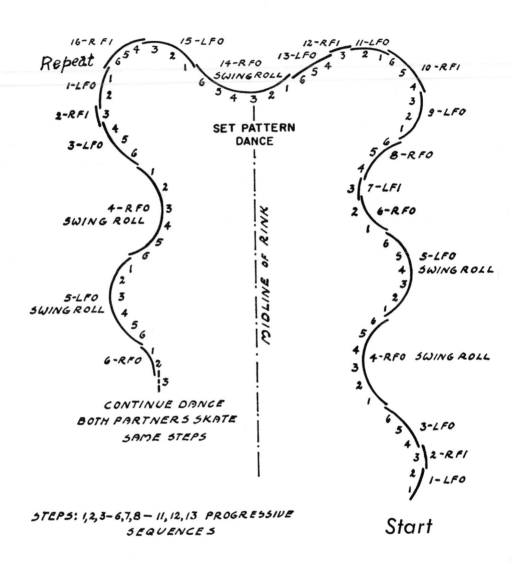

STEPS: 1,2,3 – 6,7,8 – 11,12,13 PROGRESSIVE
SEQUENCES

Diagram 11   Dutch Waltz

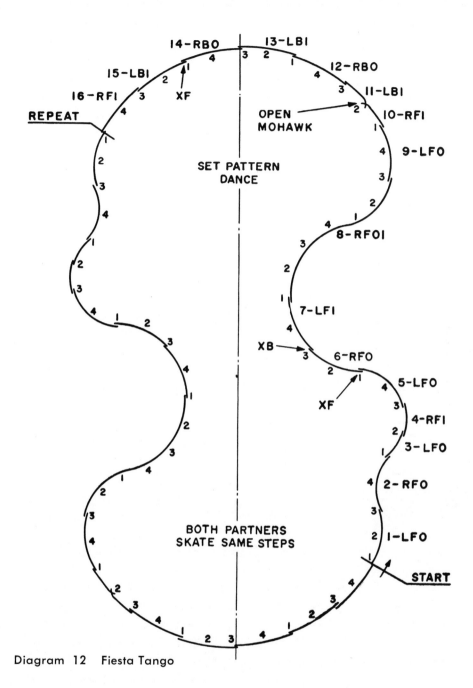

14-RBO 13-LBI
15-LBI 12-RBO
16-RFI 11-LBI
XF 10-RFI
OPEN
MOHAWK
REPEAT 9-LFO

SET PATTERN
DANCE

8-RFOI

7-LFI

XB 6-RFO

XF 5-LFO
4-RFI
3-LFO
2-RFO

BOTH PARTNERS
SKATE SAME STEPS 1-LFO

START

Diagram 12   Fiesta Tango

end and starting the repetition from the corner diagonally opposite the start (Diagram 11). It is well to count the musical
beats, at least until you are thoroughly familiar with each
dance. Here the progressive stroke comes on an unaccented
beat, the third, and as this is what keeps the rhythm from becoming unpleasantly monotonous, do not miss it. Concentrate
on co-ordinating the bend and rise of your skating knees, as
well as the extension and swing of your free legs. Do not watch
your partner's feet. Look up and look happy!

FIESTA TANGO

This, too, is a side-by-side dance in which the partners exe-
cute the same steps at the same time, but it has a turn involving
a slight change of position and more rhythm variation to make
it exceedingly enjoyable. It is outlined in Diagram 12.

The man is this time on the lady's right at the start, in the
same position as in the Dutch waltz but on the opposite side
holding opposite hands. Count the tango tempo carefully and
make sure you stay on the beats indicated in the diagram, as
this is what gives the dance its distinctive character. Two or
four introductory strokes of two beats each will serve to get you
both under way. Again start in one corner and progress lengthwise down the side and across one end before repeating the
whole sequence.

Points to watch with care are:

1. Distinct *outside* edges at the start.

2. Clear cross step forward and cross behind following the
first progressive.

3. Synchronized swing of the free legs plus a bend, rise, bend
of the skating knee on the six-beat change of edge (you both
may, if you like, turn your heads back as you swing your legs
back, to give a bit of elaboration here).

4. The lady should move slightly ahead on the next LOF
step preparatory to quick one-beat timing of the open mohawks.

5. Neat shift of hand and arm position to the lady's opposite
hip during the mohawk as she remains on the man's right and
on the inside of the curve while doing the back strokes across
the ends of the ice.

6. Again a neat shift of position back to the original side-by-side hold after the back crossover (step 15) as you make the transition to the final RIF before repeating.

Properly done, this dance has a nice feeling of edge and lilt. On the cross steps and the change of edge there is a good opportunity for real knee rhythm. Let your bodies lean and your edges flow—and don't forget for an instant that this is a *tango*. Put as much tango expression as possible into your movements.

FOURTEEN STEP

Skated to 6/8 or 4/4 time, this is a bright dance—and it is the first one you have encountered where the partners do different steps. It is skated in regulation ballroom position, with the lady starting backward facing the man. So the first thing to learn is a start (Diagram 13) that puts the lady in place for the opening steps.

Stand side by side, the lady on the man's right, his right hand clasping her left. Both stroke a ROF roll (4 beats), with the man making sure he follows his partner (his tracing tracking hers) as they swing their free legs forward. Now, with the lady out ahead, they both step LOF (toward the barrier—or ice edge) for one count. On count 2 of the music the lady turns a LOF three to LIB, while the man takes a RIF.

On counts 3 and 4 the lady steps ROB and the man LOF while the lady, who is now facing the man, places her right hand in his left. She now does a LOB roll and he a ROF roll for four beats during which they close in to regular dance position; that is, the man slips his right hand behind the lady's back, placing it firmly between her shoulder blades; she rests her curved left elbow on his raised, curved right elbow and places her left hand against the front of his right shoulder in such position that she can exert pressure against him through her left arm (this is one of the ways the partners maintain an equidistant, parallel position throughout the dance); the man meanwhile strokes directly in front of and close to the lady, holding out his left, or guide, arm at a comfortable height, with the elbow neither rigidly straight nor yet crooked.

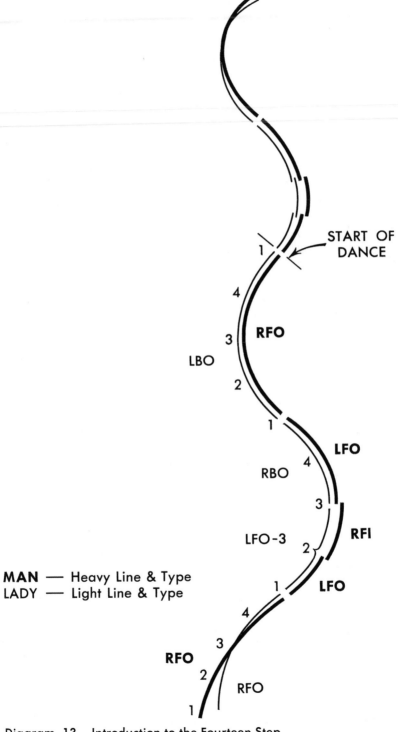

START OF
DANCE

1

4

3 **RFO**

LBO

2

1

4 **LFO**

RBO

3

RFI

LFO-3

2 **LFO**

1

4

3

RFO

2

1 RFO

MAN — Heavy Line & Type
LADY — Light Line & Type

Diagram 13   Introduction to the Fourteen Step

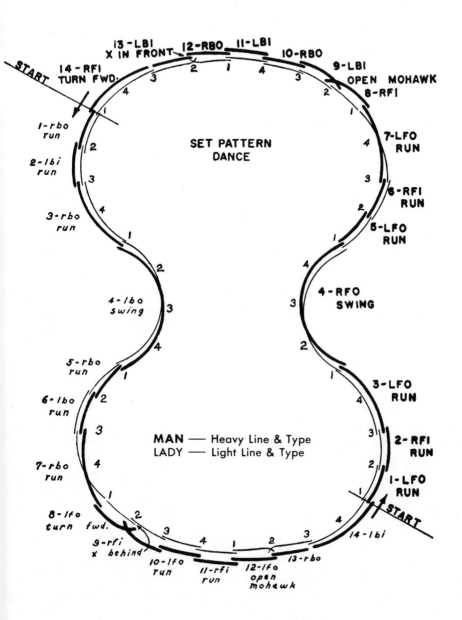

Diagram 14   Fourteen Step

After this final roll (man ROF, lady LOB) curving toward the barrier, you are both ready to start the dance proper (see Diagram 14). As this introduction is used for many different dances, it is wise to work on it separately until all your footwork and timing is neat and your placing comes automatically. Of course you realize that, as in ballroom dancing, facing partners match their footwork by stepping always on opposite feet. Thus the lady's first LOB corresponds exactly to the man's ROF, etc.

On studying the diagram, you will at once discover that the man's part is the same as the ten-step we learned back in chapter III, with a few minor variations in foot placement and the addition of a three-step progressive sequence and a ROF roll. Four steps plus 10 equal 14—hence its name. Simple, isn't it? The lady's part, as is often the case, is considerably more difficult than the man's, which is no more than justice considering that he must do the leading, often under crowded conditions. And he *must* lead, and the lady *must* trust him implicitly. There is nothing more ruinous to a look of unity than a lady who is constantly turning her head to make sure she is being guided safely.

Points to observe particularly:

1. The first progressive steps must *start* toward the barrier and the roll toward center ice, so that the first progressive steps of the ten-step itself will start toward the barrier and continue in a curving pattern around the ends.

2. The lady must not turn too sharply as she goes from backward to forward on step 8, but must gauge her stroke to stay parallel to her partner's RIF preparatory to his mohawk.

3. Note step 9 is a cross *behind* for the lady.

4. All these end steps are skated with the partner's shoulders parallel to the tracings and equidistant from each other.

5. Steps 10 and 11 for the lady form a progressive sequence, and here the man exerts enough pressure on her back to draw her slightly ahead of him in order to facilitate an easy turn of her open mohawk and a neat transition to the facing position once more as she steps from ROB to LIB. This LIB is put down at the heel of the right skate which then lifts straight forward to

match the man's backward free leg on this final stroke before the repetition.

6. The roll must be skated at a good pace with a strong lean of the body to make the pattern of the entire dance come out correctly. It is also fun to add still another set of three steps, including the progressive, plus an extra roll down the side at the beginning of the dance. This turns it from a fourteen-step to an eighteen-step, which is particularly good on a large ice surface.

The swinging of the free legs on the rolls should be relaxed and perfectly synchronized but should not be so vigorous that it seems out of control. Watch the timing of the steps carefully, noting that except for the third step after each progressive sequence and the final step (all two beats each) and the rolls (four beats each), every other step is only one beat. This makes for a lively rhythm and means that soft knee action is the necessary ingredient to real flow, clean stroking, and steps that are *danced,* not walked or raced.

AMERICAN WALTZ

Of course you have been impatient to try *the* waltz. Every new skater always is. Any man who did his preliminary test waltz eight with real control is ready to learn the pattern, for the steps are identical without addition or subtraction. Ladies, however, must be sure they have truly strong OB rolls and must practice the outward transitions to OF threes on both feet before having the temerity to attempt skating them with a partner.

For I warn you: the waltz, while it is the most beguiling of all the dances, is the most difficult to perfect. The steps are simple enough, but the constant rotation of the partners around each other takes real study to control. It will probably be many sessions before you are a true expert. The waltz is a jealous taskmaster. You can not neglect it once you've started, for here, even more than with many other dances, constant practice is the road to perfection. Don't let that discourage you, however, for as you'll soon find out for yourself, constant practice is constant fun.

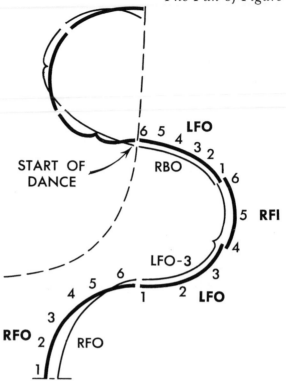

START OF
DANCE

MAN — Heavy Line & Type
LADY — Light Line & Type

Diagram 15   Introduction to the American Waltz

As the waltz is skated in the same facing dance position you just learned for the fourteen-step, you should use the same introductory steps (Diagram 15), timed differently to three-beat measures, with six beats for each roll and the lady's three turn. Thus they both stroke ROF roll for six beats, then both LOF for three beats, whereupon the lady turns her LOF three on count 4 and holds the LIB for counts 5 and 6, while the man strokes RIF on count 4 and holds it for 5 and 6. They then do another six-beat roll, lady on ROB and man on LOF.

A quick glance at Diagram 16 will show you that while the man does his three at the beginning of each lobe, the lady does a corresponding OB roll; while the man does his OB roll, the

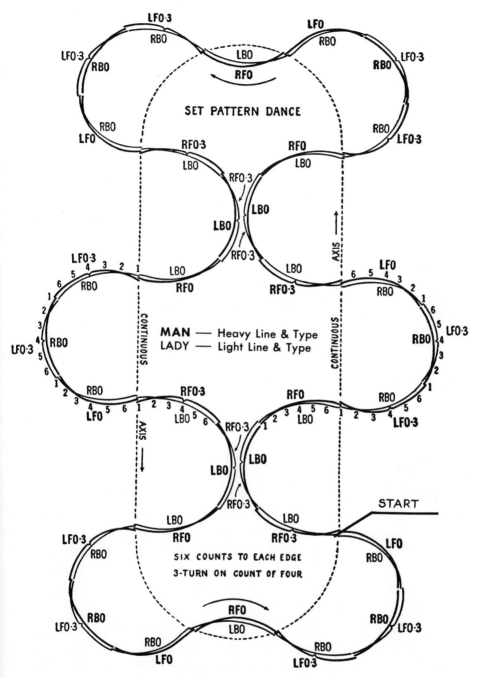

Diagram 16   American Waltz

lady turns forward and skates her three turn; while the man is finishing each lobe with an OF roll, the lady again does a corresponding OB roll. It goes without saying that all the lady's transitions from one lobe to the next are therefore done from one OB edge to the next OB edge.

Wherever the size of the ice permits, the dance should be skated in a five-lobe pattern lengthwise down each side with one six-beat roll connecting the lobes at each end. If the ice surface is very small, three lobes may be skated. As you can see from the diagram, the lobes are skated on curves of a large radius, with the three equal strokes this time forming a semi-circle (rather than the whole circle of the waltz eight). Only at the four corners are the lobes angled in such a way that they are smaller and describe more than a semicircle, so that the single six-beat edge can connect them across the ends.

Just as in the waltz eight, each stroke lasts six beats, with each new bent-kneed push on the strong count of 1 and each three turn or change of position on the weaker count of 4. The leg swings, which must be in perfect unison to bring out the full beauty of the dance, begin on count 4 and are sustained all through the counts of 4, 5, and 6 on each roll. After each three turn, the partners are both on back edges opposite and parallel to each other, with both free legs extended back at the same height and almost touching. To enable each partner to turn an easy three, the skater on a forward edge should start it slightly inside the line of the partner's backward edge, so that by shoulder rotation and a constant lean the forward edge will cross slightly outside the back edge in time to make the turn parallel to and opposite the instep of the partner's skate.

It is a prime requisite of good waltzing that the shoulders must be parallel in an absolutely equidistant body position at all times. If you don't hold your partner correctly and dance fairly close together, this is impossible. One or both of you will start pulling away in a "snap the whip" that will destroy the necessary smooth rotation into each three turn and the control of the edges before and after.

Since the entire dance is skated on curves which form arcs of circles, your knowledge of technique will tell you that your body must be held upright and both of you must lean equally toward the center of the arc the skates are making. Both partners, when starting a new lobe, must obviously change lean simultaneously in order to keep the unison not only of lean but also of the direction in which you are skating.

Once control of the edges and the placing of the lobes have been learned, it will be the use of your skating knee that will determine whether or not you look as if you are really *waltzing*. Knees that do not bend cannot rise, and so the dance becomes stiff; knees that bend but rise too fast or out of rhythm with the music turn what should be a smooth flowing movement into a bounce. The ideal is a knee bend at the start of each stroke, a gradual rise as the free legs swing in unison, and a bend again *before* the new stroke. It is this final "cushioning" bend that gives dancing softness and prevents a look of "dropping" onto a bent knee from a straight one. On the stroke that leads into the three turn, the knee rises gradually but sooner, so that at the moment of turn the skating knee is straight but not rigid and remains thus during the two-count hold after the three. This means that the partner on the OB edge must also rise a trifle sooner and time the whole swing of the free leg to coincide with the movement of the three.

In general the passing movement of the free leg is close by the skating leg with the feet almost touching; even at the three turn, although there must be no holding or other break in the rhythm, the free foot brushes past the heel of the skate at the split second of the turn. The free leg moves from the hip with no break at the knee.

For real elegance the partners must not only observe all the rules of good skating posture that I have stressed so strongly in all your skating, but must pay particular attention to the extension of the free leg both forward and backward. It should be turned out from the hip so that the inside of the free knee and foot is toward the ice on the backward extensions; the outside of the knee and foot should be turned as much as possible toward the ice (without lowering the free hip) when the free leg is in front. The free toe should be constantly pointed (press the toes down in your boot and pull your heel up), except at the moment of passing the skate.

Stroke close and softly. Use your skating knee and free leg in such harmony with the music that you feel a lilt and sway. You are doing the most time-honored dance on ice; in one form or another the "Ice Valse" has existed since the beginning of figure skating. Dances may come and dances may go, but the waltz, I'm sure, will go on as long as men and women put skates on their feet.

IX

You Are a Good Skater Now

It seems a long way, doesn't it, from your first boot fitting and your first few hesitant edges to the present moment? But think of all the fun you have had along the way and how much more fun you are going to have. For you are a good skater now.

Indeed, if you have learned to the best of your ability all the figures set forth in this book—and even a portion of the free skating and dancing—you are a very good skater. I would like to present a special graduation diploma to you, marked "Elementary Figure Skating—Cum Laude," for you are now eligible for intermediate, advanced, and graduate study of the never-ending complexities of this sport. You have a solid foundation of real knowledge from which you can go on to first-class standing; and even if you never learn another figure, you know enough now to be able to master all the dances, simple pair skating, advanced fours skating, and to hold your own in show groups, no matter how complicated.

Perhaps it has seemed discouraging once in a while and you have felt that you would never be able to do a certain edge or turn or step properly? Everyone who takes up this beautiful, exasperating, baffling, fascinating sport feels like that from time to time. There is nothing to do but persevere, practice, and above all *think* what may be the trouble. For days you may be annoyed at a stubborn figure that simply will not seem to fall into line, and just when you are about to give it all up and present your skates to the nearest urchin, you get it! It seems amazingly simple then, figure skating is the most satisfying thing in the world, and you begin your next figure with a burst of confidence. This is how it should be. This is how it will always be so long as you glide on steel runners. As you go on, you will find that a step or a jump that you could do perfectly yester-day is gone today—the timing is all wrong—and then miracu-lously tomorrow you have it again. This happens in the best of skating families. Good skating takes great stick-to-it-iveness; but wayward figures, like a wayward horse, after a period of skittish-ness always give in to a strong master.

Pair skating, as illustrated by the couple on the title page of this book, requires separate study because of the many possi-ble combinations and the specialized problems of technique in-volved. Only the most elementary remarks can be made here. It is eminently satisfying to skate in perfect harmony with another person; many people consider it the height of the skating art. But as in marriage so in pair skating, the harmony must be complete in every respect. Not only must you choose your part-ner for suitability of skating style but for temperamental com-patibility as well.

A tall, long-legged skater who covers the ice with great sweep-ing strokes should not pair with a short-legged partner whose movements are naturally quicker, "choppier," and less gliding. Similarly you should determine beforehand whether you are going to get along companionably with your partner. Argu-ments, ceaseless differences of opinion over who shall do what and why, practice squabbles and performance smiles make an unpleasant relationship which defeats the main purpose of sport, no matter how expertly two people may skate together and how much the public may like them. If skating a pair is not enjoyable in every aspect, it is not worth the trouble; on the other hand, if partners have a thoroughly good time skating together, it won't matter to them whether they win competi-tions and give frequent exhibitions or not. I know one couple who have been pair skating together several nights a week for over twenty-five years; no champions of the world could possibly have more fun on ice than this middle-aged man and woman who, having worked out over the years their own "specialties" in a highly individual style, skate them with a constant smile of pleasure on their faces.

Comparatively seldom are two skaters of absolutely equal

ability matched. While the weaker skater should strive constantly to improve, the stronger should not include in their program moves which only he or she can do confidently. A pair routine should be based on the ability of the weaker skater, for there is far more pleasure in seeing two skaters do simple moves perfectly than in sympathizing with the partner who can't seem to keep up with the other. Never, needless to say, try moves that are beyond both skaters.

Pair programs incorporate the spirals, dances, and jumps of solo free skating, plus adagio-type lifts in which the man raises the lady in graceful posed positions. The latter should be made in movement and the lift should be one continuous up-and-down motion. It should not be held so long that it seems to be merely a weight-lifting act. The lady, who generally holds her partner's wrists or his shoulder, springs and then stiffens her back and her arms while the man lifts her to a full extension and then lowers her *gently* to the ice. Pair spins should be done together as a rule. It is almost impossible for two people to spin separately for exactly the same length of time at exactly the same speed of rotation, and, as complete unity of movement is the chief essential of pair skating, anything that disturbs it should be avoided.

Dance steps may be done hand in hand, either facing as in the waltz and fourteen-step or side by side as in the fiesta tango or Dutch waltz; they may also be done by the two skaters separately, side by side, or facing, close yet not touching. If done separately, the technique is called "shadow" skating; it requires perfect timing and is highly effective if done in absolute unison, with the legs, arms, head, and body of each skater moving at the same instant at exactly the same angle. Separating moves, in which the partners go off into an individual step or jump and then meet each other in a dramatic joining, lend necessary variety to the composition. A separating figure should be so evenly spaced that the meeting seems natural and effortless yet by some subtle turn or twist the onlooker should be made to feel that there is an element of danger or difficulty involved. The separation should never be so far apart that the eye of the watcher cannot conveniently take in both skaters at once. If that happens, either one skater or the other is the focus of attention, and the feeling of unity is lost.

Much dancing with your partner is excellent pair practice, and so is the side-by-side practicing of all the rolls and even of elementary figures. The rhythm of perfectly timed steps and arm movements is the chief beauty of pair skating, and both dancing and school figures are excellent means to this end. A program is most enjoyable when both skaters have a hand in composing it; yet in the actual skating the lady must always follow the man (even if he's wrong!) with seemingly no will of her own. A pair in which the lady looks as if she is putting her partner through his paces is a jarring sight.

Figure skating competition is open only to members of the United States Figure Skating Association in juvenile, novice, junior, and senior divisions for singles contests; junior and senior divisions for pairs. Age is a qualifying factor *only* in the juvenile class, where skaters twelve years of age (or under) who have passed their 2nd test may enter. In all other classes only the passing of higher tests is a prerequisite, with the Gold Medal test a requirement at the national senior level.

The annual skating club carnival, gymkhana on skates, or whatever the ice show may be called, is an integral and enjoyable part of most club schedules. Even if you do not earn a starring role, the graduate of this book has sufficient skill to take part in any of the group numbers that form the back-bone of such a show. In fact, you are qualified for such a part in one of the many touring professional ice shows that have been popular over the country for the past twenty-five years. Many a young skater finds this an enjoyable way to earn a good living while seeing the country and indulging in his favorite sport at the same time.

Group skating, whether in the advanced category of mixed fours, eights, and twelves, or in the relatively elementary class of drills, large dance ensembles, etc., demands above all an ear for the beat of the music and a sense of "guiding" to keep your place by regulating the length of your stroke to the others.

There is great satisfaction in being an integral part of a moving rhythmic whole that glides over the ice in perfectly timed formations.

All skating is becoming more and more interpretive. I foresee the day when hundreds of expert skaters, not just a few super-stars, will, by their mastery of ice movement and mimicry, be able to evoke in the onlooker the same emotions as the other forms of dance art—when choreography on the ice stage will hold its own with any other stage.

For this reason I advocate that any talented child who decides to run the gamut of figure skating competition from the preliminary test to the Gold Medal should add the study of music and of all forms of dance to the study of skating. To the parents who constantly ask me about supplementary ballet for their children, my answer is invariably, "Yes, but *correct* ballet, and they must learn to *skate first.*" A child should acquire the "feel of the ice," with a real glide and a "soft" knee, before any other type of movement is superimposed.

Whatever category of skater you may be when you have completed the grammar school course this book comprises—recreational, club, or competitive—there are still more fields to conquer, more figures to learn, more steps to work out, more spins, more glide and assurance to gain, more style, more poise, more *fun.*

As the seasons slide by, you will try to learn always more about this inexhaustible subject of figure skating. You may not be able to do everything; but you will surely want to *know* as much as possible. There is one rule that seems to apply to every one of us who takes up the "art sport" in all its many aspects: Once a skater, always a skater.

About the Author

MARIBEL VINSON OWEN was born in Winchester, Massachusetts and graduated *cum laude* from Radcliffe College. She held the North American Singles championship for a number of years and has been the North American Pair Champion as well as a member of three U.S. Olympic Figure Skating Teams. Mrs. Owen has the distinction of having been the first woman sports writer on the *New York Times*. After her newspaper experience she returned to skating as a professional and toured the country with her own show.

Her popular skating classes and her coaching work with such champions as Tenley Albright and her own two Olympic Team daughters have won for Mrs. Owen an international reputation as a figure skating teacher. She has taught over 4,000 pupils—from housewives and businessmen to six members of the latest U.S. Olympic Team.

Set in Linotype Baskerville
Format by Seamus Byrne
Manufactured by American Book-Stratford Press
Published by Harper & Brothers, New York